Nonsynch:

A Handbook for Working with Difficult People

A working handbook designed to help people learn to interact positively with others in a professional setting anywhere.

Kathy Tuten

Introduction

This is a handbook designed to help people learn to work with others in an office, a department, a school, a factory, a classroom.

Over the years in my capacity as a trainer of teachers, assistant principals, principals, district office staffs, superintendents, and school boards, and even in the business world teaching company trainers on a national level I discovered that the one element common to all of the people I worked with is wondering how to deal with people who exhibit very difficult behavior in a normal office or classroom setting. As my training duties reached the state and then the national level, I still found that people most often expressed major concerns about others in their office who were really hard to work with. They were hard to converse with. They didn't complete their tasks well or on time. They yelled at other people. They spread gossip. They dumped on others frequently and out loud in front of other people.

Sometimes these folks don't impact the office atmosphere or work quality of others much at all, but sometimes they make everyone around them miserable. When one person can sour the atmosphere in a whole group of people who must work together, it is a given that the quality of work will eventually suffer.

So I've put together a very informally written, very clearly written, but heavily researched, handbook to help people with 'people problems' in their workplace. This is actually a workbook, with spaces to complete to help think about how to handle these Difficult People (DPs).

This is *not* a scholarly treatise on people with emotional problems and how physicians would help them. It is a handbook of concrete, practical information on what these people look like and how they behave in an office setting. And concrete suggestions for what normal people can do with them to make everyone's workplace a better place to be for eight, or ten, or more hours.

The point of the Workspace pages is to get *you* to think about what you're facing *before* you tackle a DP, or before you react—badly—to a DP who's on your case. Yes, the Workspaces take some time, but my point is that it's worth taking time to think things through, look at yourself, and then make a concrete plan for what you want to see in the future from this person. If you have a particular DP in your office, take the time to complete the Workspace, even if you think you don't *have* the time! These ideas *will* work if you do a little homework.

At the end of the handbook you'll find a Resources section, with some extra Workspace forms and ideas, and a Bibliography of some relevant, important books, if you want to do some of your own research.

We all spend entirely too much time in a professional work setting to have to live miserably for a number of years. So grab you courage with both hands, and go for it!

Table of Contents

Section 1:Some General Help

1. Why Me and Why Now? p.9
2. What Do Difficult People Really Look Like? p.12
3. Look at Yourself Too p.16
4. Problem Solving p.18
5. Sustaining Difficult Behavior p.22
6. Is Change Really Possible? p.27
7. Time Robbers p.30
8. Crises p.35
9. Depression? p.38
10. Excuse, Ignore, Collude p.41
11. Some General Problem Solving Help p.47
12. Problems, Problems p.55
13. YOUR Fault p.59
14. Mental Games p.65
15. Policies p.68
16. Stand Up! p.73
17. Fight or Run Away p.77

Section 2: Specific Kinds of Difficult People

1. Absolute Control Freak p.83
2. Bad Job! p.87
3. Boasters p.90
4. Bossy Explosions p.93
5. Bully Bosses p.96
6. Chewing the Fat p.99
7. Cliques p.102
8. Criticism, Criticism p.106
9. Hard Headed p.109
10. I Just Can't Seem to Get There on Time... p.112
11. I Know It ALL! p.114
12. I *Look* Good But..... .... p.117
13. Just Following Orders p.120
14. Liar, Liar p.123
15. Nitpickers p.127
16. Oh, My, Oh, My, Oh, Sigh.... .... p.131
17. Passive-Aggressives p.135
18. Rumor Mongers p.139
19. Snoops & Tattletales p.143
20. Special Cases: Yellers p.146

21. The Chronic Time Policeman p.150
22. The Cons p.154
23. The Dumper p.157
24. The End-around (or, Just Leave Me Alone till I Can Retire) p.160
25. The Exploding Colleague p.163
26. The Persecutor Boss p.165
27. The Rescue Problem p.171
28. The Sneaky Ones p.176
29. Verbal Abuse p.181

Resources: Worksheets, Scenarios, Blank Plan Sheets

1. Worry Check Sheet p.187
2. My Action Plan p.189
3. Practice Scenario One p.191
4. Practice Scenario Two p.192
5. Notes to Self p.193
6. Partnership Agreement Sheet p.194
7. Work Plan p.196

References

About the Author

Section 1:

Some General Help

Why Me and Why Now?

Very first point: difficult people have a *predictable*, abrasive style of behavior. They truly have a character disorder. They think, "Life is out of synch, not me...." They are experienced as 'difficult' by most people, not just you. Right off the top of your head, who do you know right now who fits this picture?

Difficult people surround us in the worksite, the department store, the school, the church. I've had many years dealing with difficult people and studying how to work with them so that we both get our needs met. I'm not a psychiatrist, but I have studied intensively the literature, and I've been there and done that with most varieties of difficult people. I've seen lots of websites about 'dealing' with difficult people but the tips they offer are very general in nature. They say things like, "have an action plan", but they don't tell you what that plan should or could look like. Or they say "the person could just be having a bad day" but they don't tell you what *that* looks like, as opposed to a person who exhibits the characteristics of the truly psychologically difficult person. Or they tell you "examine your own attitude before you confront someone you suspect might be a difficult person." But they don't tell you what *that* means. How do you do this? How do you look and act when you have examined your own attitude? And the one I like the best: "Just walk away." Well, what if you *can't* just walk away? What if your supervisor is this person? Or what if your difficult person is the big boss? You can't just walk away from either situation, no matter how much you want to.

So what I intend to do is describe what difficult people really look like in their behaviors, and offer concrete suggestions about what concrete actions you can take in a number of different situations when you find yourself face to face with someone who makes you doubt your own sanity. Unlike other books I have found on the subject of conflict in the workplace or solving problems in the workplace, this is a workbook, not just a list of generic suggestions to get you started. I want to give you concrete *behaviors* for you to use if you are struggling with a difficult person. I also want you to have a 'workspace' where you can make notes for yourself on different ways to behave or different behaviors you want to see from a difficult person, and then a place for you to react and respond after you've tried a technique, so you can reframe your behavior the next time, or save your success for future reference.

The book is divided into two sections. Section 1 provides you with a general picture of what difficult people look like, and how they typically behave in your office/department/school (classroom?). This section also offers you some general kinds of concrete actions you can take to help you deal with a difficult person. I also suggest you take a look at yourself and work through some steps you can take to get a handle on your own reactions to a difficult person.

Section 2 goes into more detail on the most common types of difficult people you find around you and gets more specific on how you identify each one, and on behaviors you need to exhibit when working with each kind.

After each chapter in both sections there is a 'Workspace' where you can make your own notes, to use the next time you face a difficult situation.

<u>Why Me and Why Now Workspace</u>

One person I know	Behaviors I find difficult to deal with:
Describe (don't name), this could be anyone you know, not necessarily just someone in your office :	<u>**1.**</u> <u>**2.**</u> <u>**3.**</u> <u>**4.**</u> <u>**5.**</u>
Who else finds this person difficult?	**How do I usually react when confronted with this person?**
	Describe:

What would I *like* to see from this person?	Notes to Self:

What Do Difficult People Really Look Like?

And how do they act that clues you in to the fact that they are not just having a bad day?

It doesn't take but one person in any kind of an office setting, or even if you are one of those professionals who telecommutes frequently with a group of colleagues, to ruin the atmosphere for everyone around her. Most people may have bad days occasionally or more than occasionally but you know they are generally pleasant to work with and not hard to deal with when you must work with them. And you can easily identify the source of her upset.

On the other hand, there is the person who is frequently or always having a bad hair day! This is a truly 'Difficult Person.'

But how do you tell the difference? Learning to tell the difference may not sound like a terribly important skill, but it could help you survive in a dysfunctional office, a dysfunctional colleague, a dysfunctional boss, a dysfunctional direct report. How you respond to a Difficult Person is a skill that can be learned to your advantage, but first you need to know what a DP looks like in your presence in order to know how to respond to them. What attitudes and behaviors do you see in your office?

First thing to think about is what kinds of attitudes do most people in your office exhibit on a good day? On a bad day?

How do they behave in general? When the boss comes down on them? When one of them screws up an assignment? When a large assignment doesn't get done on time? Usually, people pull together in any of these situations. There's no blame passed around. No one is hung out to dry. No one makes excuses. And when a major assignment is complimented by the big boss, the office wins a major grant that took months to write, a major presentation before hundreds goes down incredibly well, everyone shares in the good news. No one claims all the credit, no one takes all the congratulations for herself.

However, there may be a DP in your midst (hopefully, only one!) who manages to sour everything, even the good stuff. What does a DP really wants from her job, regardless of her position in the hierarchy? What she really wants is to do her own thing, whenever she wants to do it, and she doesn't want anyone messing with her. Good grief! How do you handle this? No one can realistically get away with all of these demands, but they sure can try! And they try by making everyone else's professional life miserable.

Here are some things to think about as you begin to deal with a DP in your office. There's a lot of emotional baggage tied to a DP's personality, baggage that you unfortunately have no control over, but you get the benefit of anyway.

1. DPs have spent most of their lives getting exactly what they want when they want it. As children they were so difficult to get along with that the path of least resistance for their parents was to just give in more often than not. So as adults they don't have any way of knowing that how they are behaving is causing problems for everyone else, or that their behavior might be totally inappropriate to the situation.

2. What happens to exacerbate their 'difficult' behavior is that they spend their adult life being miserable because they can't always get their way, so they figure that if they are miserable everyone else might as well be miserable too.....

3. So, DPs don't really have any inclination to change their behavior for the good of others because they don't even really see that they are behaving badly. They are behaving like they always do, the way they have behaved since childhood. The attitude they project is, "This is who I am, deal with it."

4. DPs often get themselves into a situation they originally thought was going to show off their talents, but when they get into it they decide they really don't like it (it turns out to be more difficult or more time consuming than they thought or it turns out not to be of star-making potential), so they spend hours and hours griping and moaning and complaining about it to anyone who'll listen-or even people who are trying very hard NOT to listen.

5. Some DPs think that everything in the office, everything at home, life in general is a competitive sport, and they are in competition with everyone they know regardless of the task, the meeting, the situation. They are determined to 'win out' at any cost. They are going to defeat you and all your colleagues at whatever they can because that means they 'win.' Remember that slogan about whoever dies with the most toys wins? This is similar in that whoever screws over the largest number of other people in the shortest amount of time wins.

6. DPs are often verbally abusive to everyone they come into contact with. That way they can then keep a problem away from themselves and therefore have a whole cadre of other people to blame if something goes wrong.

7. DPs frequently try to bring the problem you are having with them to a personal level and not a *good* personal level either. You, poor thing, get sucked into a vicious circle of name calling, insults, put downs, before you even recognize you've been had! The DP shifts the problem away from herself very slickly by starting to tell you YOU'RE the person who's impossible to deal with, because you set an unrealistic timeline, you didn't give her enough information to do the job well, the person you assigned to work with her is lazy and good for nothing. In other words, it's all your fault. And guess what happens when you start retaliating in kind? You lose! Once the conversation deteriorates into personal accusations you've lost the thread of your conversation about the problem itself!

What Do Difficult People Really Look Like? Workspace

General attitudes in your office:
Describe:

What does a good day look like in your office?
Describe attitudes and behaviors:

What does a bad day look like in your office?
Describe attitudes and behaviors:

How do people react when the boss comes down on them?
Describe:

How do people generally react on successful completion of a big task?
Describe:

Is there anyone in your office who most people seem to have concerns about?

Describe (don't name) what makes him/her hard to work with. Use the seven descriptors in this chapter to help you with your description.

Is there anyone in your office who exhibits more than one of these behaviors?

Describe (don't name) this person's behaviors in general:

How do you and your coworkers generally respond to this person?

Describe how you and your coworkers generally respond/react to this person:

Notes to Self:

Look at Yourself Too

There are some difficult truths about yourself that you will have to wrestle with before you begin to deal with a DP in your office, whether you're the boss, a colleague, or you report to a DP. These are aspects of your own (normal) personality that you need to really think about before you tackle a DP. Don't just blow off this section. Really think about the issues here. These are hard to get your brain around sometimes but you need to do some deep thinking on each one of them.

Think about this tough one first and then look inside yourself:

You can't ignore someone else's difficult behavior unless you don't really mind if it happens again. Huh? Sounds like I'm trying to pass the blame onto you. But really turn this around and around inside your head. If someone else is causing you difficulty in your workplace, and you're putting up with it, and it's causing you to do less than your best work, do you want this situation to last until you have ulcers, or you're sitting in a corner talking to yourself? If not, then it's your business to fix the problem, not someone else's.

Next, think about this hard truth:

The rest of us frequently become enablers. We cover up for DPs when they've done a bad job on a report. We make excuses for them when they don't get a presentation done on time. Or we just flat out lie for them when they didn't do their part of a group assignment. Why do we do that? It's less trouble and fewer feathers will get ruffled if we just muddle through. Know anyone like this?

The reverse of enabling is this: you can't make anybody do anything if they are willing to take the consequences. The woman who is constantly 10 minutes late for work may not care if she gets written up each time she's late, but she knows she's so good at what she does, and that she'll keep getting away with her extra 10 minutes. Know anyone like this?

Remember: you are responsible only for your own behavior, not anyone else's. You probably report to someone else and therefore you are responsible *to* someone else but you are not responsible *for* anyone else or their behavior.

You are a very nice person and hope that your colleagues and your boss do their jobs well because it's the right thing to do. However, being nice can have its drawbacks when you're trying to help a DP solve a problem. Here's something to remember about yourself. You cannot draw a change of behavior line gradually. It won't solve the problem, and may even exacerbate it. So you can't negotiate with the person who comes in 20 minutes late; you can't say, "I'll give you fifteen minutes every day this week and then 10 minutes every day next week," etc. Yes, you are trying to be nice, but that won't solve the problem. You must be firm in your expectation. There's an old saying that all benefits become expectations. So if you're going let your DP slide a few minutes here and there, you haven't solved the problem at all. And, in this case, that's your fault.

Look at Yourself Too Workspace

This is a workspace for you to do privately. If there's more than one DP in your life, you may want to complete more than one of these sheets. Don't feel any obligation to share with anyone else; this is for you to take an honest, clear look at your own behaviors when confronted with a DP in your life.

When I'm Around a Person I Find Difficult I Usually:
Describe your reactions to a DP:

Have I Ever 'Covered Up' for Someone Else's Mistakes?
If 'yes' why and what happened:

Have I ever Ignored Someone Else's Temper Tantrum, Bad Behavior?
If 'yes' why and what happened:

Have I Ever Let Someone Slide for Bad Behavior?
If 'yes' why and what happened?

Have I Ever 'Fudged' for Someone Else?
If 'yes' why and what happened?

Problem Solving

Difficult people are terrible problem solvers. We, on the other hand, end up being neurotic about their problems. We end up blaming ourselves for not being able to get along with them. We are neurotic because neurotics are mostly good problem solvers but then again we neurotics believe all problems <u>can be solved!</u>

Well, guess what: we can't solve the problems of the difficult person, mostly because their problems have nothing to do with us. We just suffer from the fallout from their problems. What you CAN do when faced with a difficult person who is in the midst of some problem that seems insurmountable to him is to do some old fashioned reflective listening. It goes something like this. Difficult Person slams into your office and slams down a folder right in front of you.

Difficult Person: The boss just gave me this ridiculous project to do. It absolutely can't be done in the amount of time she gave me. It's just too haaaaard... She's always giving me this kind of stuff to do and then she comes down on me when it's not done on time. **YOU**: What's the problem?

DP: I have to put together a spreadsheet on our top twenty accounts, and I have to have it ready by Mondayyyyy I just can't do it.

You : Why do you think you can't put it together?

DP: This is so stupid. She's just picking on me. How do I know what our top 20 accounts are? Top 20 in what??? I've got to include so much information it will come out to 14 different categories I have to include. It's impossible!

You: Why don't you go down to the Accounting Office. I'll bet they can give you the top 20 accounts in dollars spent with us in 5 minutes. That'll at least give you some place to start.

DP: Yes, but I still have to have all this other information on them? What the heck am I supposed to do about that?

You: why do you think 14 categories are so hard?

DP: She knows I have a hard time setting up a spreadsheet! (Notice, DP is deflecting the problem away from himself, typical of DPs; he's blaming his problem on the boss.) **(Meanwhile, DP's voice keeps rising, and he's starting to spout steam)**

You: Is it putting together the spreadsheet or getting the information for the columns that's giving you pause?

DP: Well, actually it's deciding how to decide the categories to go into the spreadsheet.

You: Well, here's a suggestion. Why don't you just think about maybe the largest chunks of information first? Does what you need fall into some major categories? **DP**: Hmmmm. Actually, now that I look at it I think I see maybe three big ones.

You: Well, why don't you start with those three and then once you get into the information, you might find those three big ones break out all the rest you need. And so on.

Notice: One thing you *did* was to reflect back to the DP what he was saying while still keeping calm. Reflective listening keeps the other person focused on the issue at hand and helps him clarify-at least-and get to the real root of the problem-at best. In this case you're helping him see that it's not the boss picking on him that's got him so upset; it's that he can't immediately get a handle on how to divide up a lot of information into sections that make sense. And one thing you *didn't* do. You didn't offer to take on part of the problem so you could try to solve <u>his</u> problem. Remember, it's not your problem. You've probably got more assignments than you can handle yourself.

<u>Problem Solving Workspace</u>

Now it's time to practice your problem solving skills and your reflective listening skills. How would you talk to the local DP when she storms into your office with the following problem?

DP: OMG! I don't know how I'm going to do this! Listen to this! I just got handed this ridiculous report to do on language learning products! I don't even know where to start! How many of these programs are out there, anyway! How am I supposed to compare them when they're so different from each other??? Can you help me?

Notes to Self:

<u>Sustaining Difficult Behavior</u>

We need to be aware that we create and sustain difficult people's behaviors every time we give in to them instead of confronting them. They learn very quickly that they can get whatever they want by simply manipulating us into accepting their behavior. What you need to think about is the fact that you are being manipulated by someone whose self-esteem is already low. And eventually, if you let it go on long enough, your own confidence starts to erode. And you get caught in a vicious circle of backing off and therefore giving permission for bad behavior.

Let's follow an extended example: the employee who is consistently late for work, probably two or three times a week. Not by much, just enough to have to have someone fill in for her. You, the boss, say to her, "I'm going to write you up the next time you're late." The next time she's late, which is probably only a couple of days later, she has a wonderful, teary eyed excuse, so you say, "OK, I'll let you have this one. But don't do it again." Guess what, you just gave her permission to be late any time she wants to be.

Even worse, one person is frequently late to work, and you, the boss, rather than sitting her down for a good talk, start requiring *everyone* to sign in in the morning. Guess what, rather than solving your one problem, you now have fifty employees angry with YOU, not her any longer. And I can tell you that she has no problem signing in--late--that only aggravates all the conscientious employees who are on time every day. There are also those DPs who sign in with a manufactured time; they can immediately subtract those minutes they were really late and put a phony time right in black and white. You can be standing there looking right at them and unless you confront them right there, the sign in sheet carries no weight. They gamble, probably successfully, that you can't be there all the time and wait while everyone signs in, and you're not going to confront them in public, so they get lucky.

Then there's the person who can't ever seem to get to a meeting on time. I know a lot of people don't like meetings but in many circumstances meetings are important to pass along information or to seek input. What you don't want to do is require the whole office/department/staff to sign into meetings. What you do instead is start the meeting on time; that respects the effort of the people who are there at the appointed time, and if the DP misses important information, that's her problem. Don't wait for her. That gives her permission to be late and just irritates everyone else.

On the other hand, it's the *boss* who's always late for her own called meetings. That's to show you that she's way more important than you are.... You obviously can't call her out, most likely, so solve your part of the problem by bringing some office work to do-things that don't call for heavy thinking; maybe some of those routine things you hate to take time away from more important things to do. Or, bring a book to read. Or have that collegial conversation with a coworker you don't get to spend much time with, but would like to. In any event, turn this kind of manipulation into something positive that will keep you out of trouble, and as a bonus get some serious work done rather than twiddling your fingers and silently fuming.

What you need to remember is the fact that you are being manipulated. And eventually, if you let it go on long enough, your own confidence starts to erode.

The solution is to follow through on what you say. If you tell someone you're going to write her up, write her up! If you tell someone you will dock her pay, dock her pay! If you tell someone, you will formally discipline her, formally discipline her. Only by following through will you stop being manipulated.

And remember that difficult people are terrible problem solvers. Even before you get to the writing up, try helping the person solve her problem. Set some time aside for a conversation on the problem. Come to this meeting with several ideas that will solve the problem for YOU. For the one who's always late to work, maybe you want to change her schedule, so that she has to cover the territory of the person who most often has to cover for her in the mornings. Maybe you've kept an average of minutes she's late, so you add that time to her afternoon schedule.

Those are just two suggestions. But they DO work. If the person just can't stand an extra 25 minutes in the afternoon, she'll soon be showing up on time. On the other hand, she might really be OK with a revised schedule so you've still solved the problem and probably made other employees happier too.

Sustaining Difficult Behavior Workspace

A Difficult Person in your office/department:
The behavior that makes him/her difficult to work with/for:
Describe:
How you and/or your colleagues respond to her that 'sustains' her difficult behavior:
Describe your usual responses to her, and be honest: Describe your colleagues' typical responses to her:
What would have to happen in your office to eliminate this behavior?

What could you do to help eliminate this behavior?

How would you change your responses to this DP to help eliminate this behavior?

What's your plan for following through on changing your responses to this DP?

1.

2.

3.

4.

Outcome: what behavior change would you like to see with this DP?

How will you know this DP's behavior has changed for the long run?

Notes to Self:

Is Change Really Possible?

Difficult people exhibit many kinds of difficult behaviors in the workplace that you would just love to change, whether you're the boss, a coworker, or a direct report.

The problem arises when you think you can change the person herself and make her into a nicer person, more pleasant to work with. After all, you may spend more hours a day with this person than you do with your own kids.

Those of us who are not DPs think we can 'kill them with kindness' or love them and they will just see the light and reform themselves. Or we can make sure we do everything right and they will automatically learn from our example.

Well, guess what? You can't change someone else's personality, no matter how easy or difficult they are to be around. You can't change a Difficult Person's personality; you can't change anyone else's personality.

The best chance you have is to change their *behavior*. In other words, you stand a better chance of altering a DP's overt behavior, what you can see in the office. You may not be able to make major changes but there are some things you can do.

- First, understand that they don't really think about you much at all; their focus is most often on themselves and how they can benefit from any situation, good or bad. So, don't take what they say too personally. That may be hard until you get to know them and their strategies, but once you do understand you can go from there.
- Spend a bit of time on your own thinking about how best to handle this person. What is it about him that really grates on you (and probably the rest of the department too)? How would you like him to respond in each situation that you find him to be difficult?
- Come up with a plan. A plan specific to you, not everyone else who dislikes him. Specifically, maybe make a bulleted list: I'm tired of him being rude to me, so I want him to.... When he insults me, I want him to..... When he hands in the third report late, I want him to..... Understand that this plan focuses on you and what you will do to 'educate' him on how you want him to respond to you, not on what he should do or should want to do. He doesn't really care what you want him to do, but you care about how you want him to respond. That's why a plan comes in handy. That way you are less likely to lose your temper, start yelling, or laying into him, none of which will work, and might get you fired to boot.
- Be kind to this person or at least as kind as you can be. It's always flattering to people when you ask about their family, how's the report coming, how's your dog. That's probably not going to get rid of obnoxious behavior, but it will probably ameliorate it some. After all, you are showing you care about them whether they care about you at all. It'll sure make you feel better anyway. Think about that.
- Always deal in facts, not opinions or feelings. Always, always, always. That takes personalities out of problems and will at least make you feel like you have more control over the situation.

Is Change Really Possible Workspace

Pick ONE behavior or attitude this DP exhibits that really bothers you. Focus on ONE thing at a time. If this person exhibits more than one difficult characteristic, use one Workspace for each characteristic.

Remember that this Work Plan focuses on you and what you want do when faced with this person.

Think about a Difficult Person you know. What is the ONE thing about him/her that really grates on you?
Describe:
How would you LIKE him to respond to you?
Describe:
Work Plan:
1. I'm tired of him being:
2. So I want him to:
3. When he_____:
4. I want him to:

5. The next time he_____:

6. I am going to:

Notes to Self:

Time Robbers

Difficult people are robbers of your time and energy. Believe it or not, they take up 40 to 60% of your time even if they are not physically with you. They don't necessarily have stress themselves, but they sure are carriers.

Think about it. If it's your boss who's the difficult person, how much time do you spend both in the office and out of the office worrying, worrying, worrying. In the office you worry about when you'll get the next laying out by the boss. You sit in your cubby and dread the next meeting, the next assignment, the next report. When is the boss going to show up at your door next to tell you what a lousy job you're doing, how you could have done your last assignment so much better, what a general waste of time you are. At home you go back over and over and over the argument you had with the boss right before you left the office, an argument you didn't start, by the way. You sit over dinner and start worrying about how to confront him in the morning to go through your side again, or if you should just suck it up and take it again, or even if you should get out on the pavement and look for another job. You go to bed with your stomach in knots and your head screaming and you wake up the next morning not a whole lot better. If you think about this scenario and it sounds all too familiar to you, just think about all the work you're *not* getting done during the day, all the conversations with your spouse, all the playing with your children in the evening you're *not* participating in. And think about how you're shortening your own life!

If this is your boss what you can do - and this takes some active practicing - is try to compartmentalize your worry. It's hard to do when you start but:

- Say to yourself, "I'm going to worry about this for thirty minutes right now." And then I've *got* to get to writing to at least page 6 of this report due next Friday.
- While you're sitting there worrying, write down every awful thing you can think of that could happen when the boss next jerks your chain. I mean *everything* both you and he could do or say that would exacerbate the situation.
- And force yourself not to do anything BUT worry for the 30 minutes.
- Fold the page(s!) up neatly and put them in your desk drawer at the end of the 30 minutes.
- Go to work on your report.
- In an hour or so, or as long as you can stand it, pull the pages out and spend 15 minutes editing or adding to them.
- Put them back in the drawer and go back to work on the report, or go to lunch, or go on break.
- Once you get used to this "scheduled worrying" you will find that your imagination is pretty much always worse than what really comes from the boss.

Make yourself some mental notes on how many hours you spend on scheduled worrying. At first I'll bet you'll be surprised at how much time you really do spend. Don't forget to do the same thing when you get home. Set aside maybe 10 minutes here and there during the evening to worry. Write everything down, and then go play with your kids or take your husband out to dinner!
What you'll discover is that once you learn to compartmentalize your boss worries, you will spend much less time on unproductive worrying and a whole lot more time on the stuff you really want to do. And that 40 to 60% worrying time will drop drastically. It's actually kind of like going to the dentist: what you imagine is always worse than what really happens.

This kind of creative worrying works as well if you're the boss and you've got a difficult employee. You probably don't like confrontation with a direct report any more than anyone else does. You may not have a 30 minute stretch in your schedule to worry, but start with 5 minutes, or 10 minutes here and there in the office. And don't forget to do the same thing at home. You may find, after several days, or maybe even weeks, the problem has resolved itself through conversations with your employee, or, on the other hand, you may have enough information to put the person on an action plan. Either way, your ulcers will bother you a whole lot less.

The point is to get to a place where you're not constantly worrying, looking over your shoulder, and dreading each day at work. "Scheduled worrying" is a good way to get a hold on your fears and knock that worrying percentage down to a much more manageable 10 to 20%.........

Time Robbers Workspace

A DP you work with/work for/who works for you:

Think for a minute. How much time would you estimate you worry about her?

What does she do/say that worries you?

Plan for 'scheduled' worrying: Step 1

How much time will you allot for worrying today? Why have you picked this many minutes?

While you are worrying, write down everything your DP could say to you the next time you have a confrontation with her. What kinds of things do the two of you have confrontations about?

-

-

-

-

-

-

-

Remember to force yourself to worry however long you said you would!

Remember to fold these sheets up and put them aside for your allotted work time

Now take your sheets and spend 15 minutes editing or adding to them. What other nasty things would your DP say to you?

-

-

-

-

-

-

File this information in a drawer or folder.

How did you feel doing this 'scheduled worrying'?

Did you stick to your allotted worrying time frame?

If not, why not?

What about scheduled worrying worked best for you?

How may minutes will you schedule for worrying tomorrow? Why this number?

Think about yourself now.
How would you like to see your own behavior (your worrying) change in the future?

Notes to Self:

Crises

One way to tell a truly difficult person from someone who is just having a bad day is to look at the crisis situation around him. Everyone has a crisis every now and then, some small and some larger than others. The difficult person is totally surrounded by crises all the time. He is in some crisis all the time! He's the man who wears a trail in the carpet between his office and your office to complain about this or that major problem. Fourteen parents have raised a negative issue with the local high school principal He couldn't find the report due today in the home office, so somebody else had it lying on their desk, or someone forgot to give it to him, or someone forgot to complete it (or complete it carefully and completely).

I think the answer to these "crises" is to think a bit about the problem, take it into your own hands where you can, and solve it. That's not nearly as hard as you think it might be if you just find the pattern to these crises. There will usually be one.

Think about reports or presentations or phone calls like these. Do these crises come with reports due at the first of the month or the end of the month? Do they come with year-end reports or end of fiscal year reports? Do "many phone calls" come with released reports to the public? Does the crisis emanate from a reporter's request for an interview about corporate earnings or test scores?

One thing you can do is ask, "Boss, if you'll give me the phone messages, I'll call each of them right now." It'll probably turn out that ONE person has called. Call that person and take care of the problem. If there really are several phone messages, ask for those pink phone notes, put them in order of priority, call them, make notes on your calls, and return your notes to the boss so she can see that you've handled the situation quickly and effectively.

You might be nervous about going through the boss's papers, but one answer to 'lost' report forms might really be to go to the boss's desk and just search through the mountains of papers, (I'll bet there are mountains!). Dig out the form you need and just quietly complete it and lay it back on his desk in an open space where he will be sure to see it.

As mathematicians are fond of saying, just look for patterns and then you'll have a good start on solutions.

Crises Workspace

Someone in your office who lives from crisis to crisis:

What kinds of crises does she usually find herself surrounded with?

Can you identify any kind of pattern to these crises?
When reports are due?
When end of the month/end of the quarter gets close?
When the Big Boss is due for inspection?
Other times?

How does this crisis behavior manifest itself?
How does she react around you and your coworkers?

How does the crisis behavior impact you and your colleagues?

How do you plan to handle this behavior in the future?
Step 1:
Step 2:
Step 3:
Step 4:

What can you do to counteract these 'crises' in the future?
Notes to Self:

Depression?

Difficult people frequently suffer from low grade, chronic depression. The problem is that they don't know they are truly depressed. They suffer from low self-esteem. Or they have a physical problem that is chronic. They are hardest to deal with when they suffer from all three.

Think about a person you're having some difficulty with. Is he constantly mumbling about how bad the world is treating him? How nobody understands him? Is he groaning more than other people in the office? Everyone has a depressing day every now and then, or even a depressing week, but every day, every day, every day is *not* normal.

Be aware that sometimes depression manifests as anger, not just a case of the blues. Is your person a match just waiting to be lit? This might show up in a meeting as the person who puts down everyone else's ideas, regardless of how anyone else feels. Frequently this is the person who insinuates little snide comments into the conversation, especially when the idea being proposed is not hers.... Or this is the "Oh, for heaven sake...Where did you come up with THAT idea?" person.

Or this is the person who just flies off the handle about a problem no one else even knew existed?

This could also be the person that hands off assignments to you frequently, because he's got another doctor's appointment for his earache, that ache he sees a doctor for probably three times a month, the one that never gets somehow gets cured.

The problem is that you're not a psychiatrist, most likely, so you can't prescribe antidepressants or conduct sessions on a couch, so what can you do?

Before you do anything else, spend some time looking for patterns in his behavior. If you find that his depression is not causing him to neglect his work or do his assignments badly or not complete his tasks frequently, then you might be wise just to set aside a few minutes a day to commiserate with him. But let him know that you have 5/10/15 minutes to listen to him (complain) and then you have to get to work. Then send him on his way with a gentle pat on the back.

If you find that his chores are beginning to slide, and if he's your coworker, and if you're sharing a task with him, write down what you are to do and what he is to do. Put steps and dates on paper. Check in with him periodically, but make sure you date and sign off on your own part of the assignment. That way you are covered if his part of the assignment goes awry.

Now, here's the hard part. If his chores are beginning to slide and you don't share tasks with him, then *it's not your problem!* Sit with him, talk to him, sympathize with him, but do *not* be tempted to pick up after him, no matter how much you like him. That doesn't solve his problem, and it will surely add to yours if you can't get your job and his job done at the same time.

Depression? Workspace

Begin to look beyond yourself at some behaviors from a DP that you are able to identify. Think about whether you are seeing signs of depression from him, start identifying what you are seeing, and start thinking about any repetitive patterns in his behavior.

Think about the difficult person you are having problems with. Do you see signs of depression?

If yes, what kinds of signs do you see:
    1.
    2.
    3.

Think a bit. Do you see any kinds of patterns to his behavior?

If yes, list and describe what you are seeing (not his attitude, but what you see):
    1.
 	
    2. In what time frame are you seeing this behavior (i.e. end of the month, when a certain regularly scheduled report is due, every day):

How is his behavior affecting his work performance, as far as you can see?
Describe:
Is his behavior affecting YOUR performance, or task completion?
1. If yes, describe specifically what you are not able to do as a result of his behavior:

2. If yes, describe what you *have* to do as a result of his behavior:

How do you find yourself responding to him?

Describe:

Notes to Self:

Excuse, Ignore, Collude

Difficult People are called difficult for a reason: they exhibit various behaviors that other people find very difficult to deal with successfully.

When faced with a difficult person one thing you *do not* want to do is excuse their behavior. What happens all too often is that their behavior is excused so often that the behavior becomes acceptable...but only for them. They would love to create new rules and new limits that apply only to them.

This is the employee who is constantly 10 minutes late for work, but you – the boss, or the team leader – don't want to confront her because she is so good at what she does. Or the boss who constantly puts employees down very cleverly, so they aren't really sure they've been insulted. Or the coworker who constantly whines and whines until you end up doing half her work. Or the employee who can never seem to get a job done on time, because it was sooo difficult and you-the boss/team leader--didn't really allocate enough time for her to complete it.

Get this point: if you continue to excuse these kinds of behaviors, then when things go wrong, it's *your fault*, not theirs. Get the picture?

The other side of excusing this kind of behavior is simply ignoring it. Unfortunately, ignoring the situation frequently causes the DP to intensify the negative aspects of her behavior. So, for example, the person who shows up for work 10 minutes late eventually starts sneaking in 15 minutes late. The boss who constantly gets little digs in on employees just for fun, starts getting in bigger digs (trust me, this does happen) more frequently. The employee who is leaning on you to do half his work begins that process earlier and earlier, so you end up doing more and more of his work and not yours. The employee who always gets an extra day to hand in reports ends up getting two extra days because she's just so overworked and she just wants to give the boss her very best work and that takes two extra days.

Some things you can do with DPs:

1. First, stay calm; hard to do maybe but it will stand you in good stead in the long run.
2. For someone who is time challenged, if you're the boss, put her on a plan of action and be sure you follow through. No ifs, ands or buts. Document. If you're a coworker, make your feelings known pleasantly by saying something like, "I have a hard time getting the spreadsheets the boss wants done by 8:30 every Monday when I can't get the information I need from you right at 8 AM. " Document and if necessary, explain to the boss the problem you are having. No need to mention names, you're not tattling. You just need to make known the fact that you can't get the boss's wishes taken care of if you can't get appropriate information fed to you in a timely manner. Enough said.
3. If it's the boss who is being insulting, even if it's slight, but it recurs constantly, make an appointment with her and let your feelings be known, without recrimination. Again, here, an old method called "I messages" works well. You say, "I feel hurt when you ..." "I get

41

upset when you..." this kind of message deflects from blaming anyone; you are talking about yourself here, not saying what you'd really love to say, like "You idiot...."

4. For a situation like the employee who is getting you to do half her work, give her a time frame to work with. Tell her you have between 3 and 4 PM this Monday and this Thursday that you will be more than happy to help her. Otherwise, you are tied up with your own work. Don't lie about your workload just to get her off your back! You decide how many hours you can realistically devote to her. This works really well, because, when you think about it, if her reports aren't done on time, she can't really blame you, now, can she? She will get the message pretty quickly, if you stick to your time frame.

5. In the case of the employee who constantly hands in work late, if you're the boss, document first. If you're the boss you probably already know that this person's lateness may be making other people's work late. That's something a business cannot tolerate and still remain in business. Call her in to your office and tell her what a critical part she plays in the organization and that you need for tasks to be done in a timely manner from now on. No more late days. Again, you're not focusing blame on her, because she won't respond to that. If you are concrete about the needs of other people in the department/organization, you're sticking to facts. Facts will usually work with DPs where feelings and blame won't.

What you may not realize is that excusing their behavior or ignoring their behavior is really an act of collusion on your part! You are sending subtle signals that you are OK with their bad behavior, so you can't really blame them, you need to take a look at your own behavior. I'm not saying there is ever an excuse for their bad behavior. I am saying that you need to take a firm stand to what you expect or you are complicit in the DP's bad behavior. Think about that!

Excuse, Ignore, Collude Workspace

Use this workspace to think about a DP you work with her and how you usually respond to her. Then begin designing a concrete workable plan to deal with her.

For someone you work with who is time challenged:
Describe how her behavior impacts you:

Your plan to deal with the situation:
Your specific behaviors:
1.
2.
3.
4.

What are you going to say to her?
1.
2.
3.
4.

How do you want her behavior to change as the result of your conversation?
1.
2.
3.
4.

For someone who is routinely insulting:
Describe how her behavior impacts you:

Your plan to deal with the situation:
Your specific behaviors:
1.
2.
3.
4.

What are you going to say to her?
1.
2.
3.
4.

How do you want her behavior to change as the result of your conversation?
1.
2.
3.
4.

For someone who routinely shifts her work to you:
Describe how her behavior impacts you:

Your plan to deal with the situation:
Your specific behaviors:
1.
2.
3.
4.

What are you going to say to her?
1.
2.
3.
4.

How do you want her behavior to change as a result of your conversation?
1.
2.
3.
4.

For someone who consistently completes tasks late:
Describe how her behavior impacts you:

Your plan to deal with the situation:
Your specific behaviors:
1.
2.
3.
4.

What are you going to say to her?
1.
2.
3.
4.

Notes to Self:

Some General Problem Solving Help

It is entirely possible to work successfully with difficult people in your office setting. It won't be your favorite thing to do but in these times, you'd really like to keep your job, wouldn't you? And no one ever said you have to end up liking someone who's really a problem, but you can at least learn to manage the situation to your advantage. That doesn't mean taking advantage of the DP, that's not right, but there are certainly some techniques you can use to deal with them and make sure the office atmosphere doesn't become so polluted that everyone loses.

Perhaps the major thing to remember is: *don't promise what you can't deliver.* For good or bad. Don't threaten to fire someone for his difficult behavior if you are not in the position to do the firing. Saying, "I'll get you fired!" won't work either if you're not in the position to get a higher up to do the firing. On the other hand, don't tell a direct report you'll 'take care of her' if she comes through with a well-done report. Or don't tell a colleague you'll cover for her the next time she ducks out of the office if she'll just get you her part of the group presentation. In these circumstances you will find yourself going around in circles with her. If you can't fire her, or have her fired, you lose and if you cover for her this time, she'll just do it again...and again... And you lose either way.

Before you start to work on a problem with a DP, do a little thinking about the emotional climate in the room. You can tell within five minutes if she's going to listen or not and talk rationally. It's a sure bet that if a DP won't cooperate with you, or at least give you a hearing, it's because she thinks it's to her advantage not to cooperate. So for example you tell her you'll write her up for not getting a major portion of a report in on time, and others working on the report are suffering as a result. But her husband plays golf with the Big Boss. So that won't go anywhere, and you know as well as I do that this does happen even with all the safeguards that can be thought up to prevent such things happening. So it's time to put on your thinking cap.

When dealing with a DP *stay on the problem* at hand. After you identify the emotional climate of the conversation/confrontation, what's the specific problem you need to solve? This might call on your part for what is known as 'root cause analysis.' Your DP consistently completes tasks shoddily. Although you might be tempted to think that's the problem, it's not. It's the *result* of the problem. What you need to get to is the *cause* of the problem. Sometimes problems can result from simple misunderstandings. Your colleague just really doesn't understand why deadlines are important to you. She misses deadlines over and over because she simply hasn't processed what is expected of her. The simple solution here is to set very clear goals before you start any project, whether you're leading it or you're part of a team. If you're not in charge of the team, help the team set goals anyway. I trust you're smooth enough to do this. Explain to your colleagues in detail what you want done, or what the boss wants done and why the boss wants it done this way and why he wants it done in this time frame. If you're not the one in charge, just ask the team leader if you can restate these expectations out loud so you are clear on what is needed. It is absolutely true that what seems totally obvious and simple to you may not seem obvious or simple to some other people. If it's one person only who's got the problem you'll save yourself a lot of time and grief if you pay attention to unspoken signals from her.

My suggestion here is that after the team meeting, you take her aside privately and go through the goals and tasks one by one.

One very clear thing you can do if you're dealing with a DP, is say to her, "I need to know what you want from me." When you find minor mistakes in the company's bookkeeping several times, even if you're not the boss, you no doubt walk town to the book keeper's office, or call the bookkeeper in for a talk. She whines. People come into her office frequently and distract her, and she's such a nice person she doesn't shoo them out of the office. You know you can't allow mistakes in the books regardless of what her 'problem' is. So a next step for you to correct the problem smoothly is to ask what you can do to help her. She may very well just need your permission to throw people out of her office when her end of the month reports are due. Or she may want *you* to tell people not to hang around her at the end of the month. Either way, the problem is most likely solved. If she mumbles her way through the conversation but doesn't take you up on your offer of help, and reports are again turned in with incorrect figures it's time to go to the next stage.

Another reason to stay on the problem: don't get into attitudes, either yours or the DP's. You might think you can work with his attitude, but you can't. Sorry! All you can see is his *behavior*. Take note of what you're seeing, and then think about his attitude in terms of what you are *seeing*. Define his attitude in terms of what *behavior you want to see changed*. Everyone doesn't have to sprout bluebirds every time they are given a team task. But they do need to behave, i.e. complete tasks on time, get to work on time, attend all meetings. So think about overt behavior you want to see and let go of the attitude problem.

Once you're on the way to solving a problem, don't slide into blaming anyone or anything else for the problem. If you do, you're just playing into your DP's hands. You don't want to blame the boss for this deadline, or the Big Boss. You don't want to go off on a tangent about another employee who never gets her work done on time either. You're helping your DP shift blame away from himself, and not going in the right direction yourself. State and restate, in one syllable words if you need to, what the problem is. State and restate your instructions. State and restate what behavior you want to see in future from him. And, if I were you, I'd also have those items in writing-copy with date for the DP and copy for you.

When trying to deal with a DP, offer him specific alternatives to the negative behavior he's exhibiting. This means you will need to do a little pre-work. Think about the problem you're facing, and then think about the outcome you want to see from him. Think about whether your boss would OK your alternatives; run them by him if you need to. Evaluate your alternatives in terms of your office or department budget; can you afford these alternatives? Once you've done this thinking, come up with two or three practical alternatives that he could pursue to solve this problem. Then you and he decide on the most workable alternative, and go for it! But don't neglect the follow up step for yourself: be sure to evaluate how well your alternative worked. Did the alternative work for everyone involved, or just for the DP? Did it meet your budget requirements? Will it work after this problem is on its way to being solved?

Before you meet with a DP, decide on the procedure you want to follow with her. Make yourself an agenda – a written one is the best idea because then you won't lose your own focus. If your problem simply erupts and you don't have time for a written agenda, excuse yourself for three minutes (even if you just turn around) and get an order of ideas in your mind, then go back to face your person. Always set a time limit for your listening. If you can, tell your DP what your time limit is before you even start a conversation. Time limits have a wonderful way of keeping everyone focused.

Before you meet with your DP, think about an old business truism: decide in your own mind whether this problem is urgent or important. It is absolutely true that what may be urgent is not necessarily important, but it's a problem that must be solved quickly to get other things running smoothly again. It's also the case that what's important is not always urgent. Sometimes much thought needs to go into completing a very important task and it's not urgent that it be done today.

Once you have your problem solving plan in mind, call the DP in, or sit down with her in her office, and start to work on it. However, be aware of sliding into putdowns, of the DP or anyone else. What happens if you do this is that you lose the DP's attention. DPs only want to listen to you if you have something extremely interesting or extremely crucial or critical to them. So you *have* to hold their interest. Putdowns get the wheels inside their brains going and they start immediately deflecting and get distracted and all of a sudden you're back at Square One.

Just in case you think all the help you can offer is 'Dos', here's a 'DON'T' for you. Don't ever say, "I'm sorry, but I need you to...." Why are YOU sorry if you're not causing the problem???? Enough said.

Be aware that if you put a DP on some kind of action plan, things may get worse before they get better. Once on an action plan, the DP is no longer getting her own way, and may very well try to subvert the whole plan. What you need to do is keep tight control of the steps of the action plan; don't let her slide. And stay assertive about what and when you expect her to complete each step. It helps if you keep a copy of her plan somewhere close to you, at least for a few days after it goes into effect, just so she is aware that you're up on the details.

If you're working with a DP who seems to have no real need to meet deadlines, sitting down and negotiating with her might not be workable. Instead, start with a plan you've already devised. Start with what you want her to end up with-the end point of the assignment or project, the due date – and work backwards from there. Set your own benchmarks for work along the way. One thing that works is to make a chart with all benchmarks and mini deadlines on a week by week (or day by day, if necessary) basis. Be sure to include on the chart who exactly is responsible for exactly which pieces of the project. There is power in seeing expectations in black and white. It's hard for anyone to muddle around too much when jobs are specified so clearly. Nowadays computer flow charts or dashboards take much of the work out of keeping up with timelines. They work especially well because everyone can have the same dashboard on their individual computers and can keep up with steps as they are completed.

Don't ever let a DP go unchallenged for long. If you do, her behavior will just escalate over time, and maybe faster rather than slower. What you do is keep clear and accurate notes of your experiences with a DP, with dates if possible, on what she does that is keeping others from doing their jobs well. Forget trying to appeal to her sense of fair play. That never works with these people, since they don't have much, if any.... However, be sure your notes outline the *facts,* not how her attitude is showing at the time. Remember that you can't control her attitude but you have a chance of controlling her behavior, even if you're a co-worker and not the boss. You're not 'taking names' here; if it comes to the point that you need to go over her head you will need evidence based information to share with the boss to make you case.

Some General Problem Solving Help Workspace

This workspace will help you think through behaviors and emotions you will face when dealing with a DP with whom you have been assigned a task to complete. Although you must stick to the facts only when dealing with a DP, diagnosing the emotional climate around him can help you know how to handle facts, and what facts you need to concentrate on.

A DP you work with:
Describe the characteristics you find difficult to deal with:
How would you describe the emotional climate around him?
Look at other people's body language, their facial expressions, what they say and describe:
How do you and other people *feel* when dealing with him?
How do you personally feel *after* you have had an interaction with him?

What's your plan for dealing with him the next time?
Describe your behaviors:
1.
2.
3.
4.

If you are assigned to a project with him, what will you say to him before you start?
1.
2.
3.
4.

Plan for handling yourself during your next interaction with him
List three behaviors you will monitor on yourself:
1.
2.
3.

What is the specific problem you face with him and the task at hand?
ONE specific problem. THE big problem. NOT 6 or 7 little problems. What's the ONE thing he could do/not do that will sabotage the task?

Identify in your mind what you think the *cause* of the problem is.
Why do you identify this one thing as the major problem?

What's your plan for keeping yourself on the problem?
How will you keep yourself from getting sidetracked by him and not falling into an emotional trap?

What alternatives can you offer him for completing his part of the task?
1.
2.
3.
4.

What do you want his end product to look like?
Describe what his piece(s) of the task will look like when he's finished with his part.

What's your plan to deal with him if he doesn't follow through?
In the middle of the task:
At the end of the task:

Notes to Self:

Problems, Problems

When difficult people see a problem coming, their reaction is out of proportion to the problem as it really exists. They frequently act just like 2 year olds or young adolescents: they want somebody to solve the problem for them immediately! Note that I said somebody, that means somebody *else,* not themselves, because, remember, whatever the source of the problem, it's sure not them! Therefore, someone else needs to solve the problem, NOW! Two year olds and adolescents go through a stage in which they want immediate gratification. They want everything and they want to be satisfied now; they don't have, or have lost their conception of delayed gratification. DPs, unfortunately, don't ever grow out of that stage.

If this happens to be your boss, what you'll hear, is something like, "I want this done over again and done right this time and resubmitted to me within the next hour!!!!" Or, "If you don't take care of that situation immediately, I'll have you written up!" And this reaction may come with slamming down of folders, papers flung in your face, yells from out in the corridor, stomping out of your office. You're left to wonder what in the world the problem is in the first place, and generally it's something like a chart, on one page of a 25 page report, that has one number wrong or one column wrong. If you're the 'culprit', don't take the bait. Keep focused on the problem numbers and don't grovel. If you're not the culprit, keep your focus on the problems numbers and agree to fix the problem if you can.

Or you'll hear, "In my office, NOW!" and you'll wonder what in the world you've done now. This situation can also come with ear blasting from the boss, and that could be accompanied by a recitation of everything you've ever done wrong in your whole life. If this is a boss behavior that recurs very frequently you can do a couple of things to ameliorate the situation and keep your job.

The first thing you can do is ask the boss what specifically he wants you to correct, if it's in your power to correct it, even if you had nothing to do with the problem in the first place. Stay calm. It won't make any difference if you tell the boss that you didn't commit this sin. He's so worked up he'll never hear you. Note down what he wants changed or corrected, on paper, and read it back to him to make sure you heard correctly. Then get it back within the required time, even if you have to go to a coworker (who made the goof in the first place) to get the information you need. You get the boss calmed down, you don't get anyone else into trouble, you get points, and the situation gets resolved.

The second thing you can do, if you discover that you can't solve the problem in the required time, be absolutely honest. Tell boss you need a few minutes to go through the report and figure out what needs to be done. Then tell boss that this problem is rather complex and that to do it right will take at least 5 hours (or whatever) but you will be sure to have it absolutely correct when you resubmit it. Again, you get the points and you get the situation calmed down.

If you're dealing with a coworker who is a DP, you may hear something like , "The boss just nailed me for getting wrong numbers on a chart he has to submit to his boss, and I swear I used the numbers he gave me, and I have no idea how to fix it. I am going straight to the poorhouse. You know how to fix this and you're faster than I am. How about doing it for me this time so I can take it back to the boss (*this* time?)? This request could also be accompanied by yells, tears, wheedling, chest thumping, all in an attempt to get you to get her out of trouble. Again, you've probably dealt with this person a lot.

Stay calm. Ask her what's wrong with the numbers, get her to show you the particular pages, and tell her how to fix it, if you know. Write down for her what she needs to do if there are several steps. Do *not* volunteer to fix it for her. You have your own chores to do. But do remember that you'll probably have to be working with this person for a long time, so it doesn't do you any good to get snippy, sarcastic, or dismissive to her. Your small act of kindness in giving her the answer so she can do it herself is worth the minimum biting of your tongue in the long run.

Problems, Problems Workspace

If you find yourself in an awkward position with the boss or with a needy coworker, this workspace is for you!

A DP you work for/with:
Describe the behavior(s) you find difficult:

Your plan for dealing with this behavior:

If you're the 'culprit', three things you will do to deflect this behavior:
 	
    1.
 	
    2.
 	
    3.
 	
If you're not the 'culprit':
 	
    1.
 	
    2.
 	
    3.

How will you respond if he's the boss?

How will you respond if he's a coworker?

Notes to Self:

YOUR Fault

Difficult people keep the blame for any wrongdoing or bad situation outside themselves. Life is full of problems and it's all YOUR fault! "We didn't get that contract because YOU didn't get me the information on time." Notice: you personally sabotaged the whole thing, right? You really have that power, right?

Truly difficult people themselves have never done anything wrong; there's never anything they can be blamed for when a job, a situation, a relationship goes wrong. Forget trying to say something like, "I would have gotten that report done but I didn't get the numbers in time." The answer from the boss is likely to be something like, "Well, YOU never came and asked me for any numbers." Doesn't make any difference that you asked for numbers three times and were told they weren't ready yet. That fact is conveniently forgotten.

Your coworker, a difficult person, never admits that she has given you information late, or incomplete. YOU should have had the foresight to ask her for information, or YOU should have double checked to make sure the information was complete. Doesn't make any difference that the boss assigned you a totally different piece of the project, one that has nothing to do with what your coworker was supposed to do. Your direct report is late for work three days in a row. It's her child's fault; the child just can't seem to get it together in the mornings these days. The child's fault? Who has charge of the child?

Or your direct report comes to you after a project is due and allows as to how he just never understood what it was he was supposed to do. The implication is that it is YOUR fault you never came to explain or clarify your directions.

I am frequently reminded of this trait of difficult people when I hear stories told by murderers, child abusers, spouse abusers, robbers interviewed on television. It's never their fault. It was Mother's fault. It was Daddy's fault. It was Grandma's fault. He became a murderer because he had a terrible life as a child. I don't for a minute want to downplay poor upbringings or abusive or neglectful parents, but I then wonder about all those poor and/or abused children who grew up to be outstanding citizens. These are people who readily accept responsibility for mistakes or missed opportunities.

What you do in this situation is to stay focused on the job at hand, the report, the tardiness. In the first instance, you say something like, "If you'll give me those numbers right now, or send me to the person who has them, I'll have the report on your desk tomorrow morning/this afternoon/in two hours." Don't apologize if you really tried to get the information you need. It's not your fault. But don't get all huffy...it won't do any good anyway. But do file away for future reference, who your boss sends you to to get that important information. And remember to start there the next time you get a similar assignment. Get those numbers where you can and submit the report.

In the case of your coworker, don't get confrontational; that won't work. Just document the work you were told to do, and when and how you did it, and make very sure your part of the report is completed on time. If you're done early, it wouldn't hurt to offer help to your coworker. Just don't get sucked into doing his whole part of the work. Offer to do one specific piece of the report to help out; that means ONE part. You'll get a little credit for helping, at least. File in the back of your brain that the next time the two of you are assigned to work together, put together a spreadsheet of your responsibilities and the other person's responsibilities. Put a timeline to it and mark off each step you complete with the date completed. That way you hand in your pieces of the report on time, and, if asked, you have documentation to back up yourself.

In the case of the direct report: I'm sorry, but as nice as you want to be, the child is not your responsibility. Sit down with the person and see if you can get a *specific* problem the child is having. Then give your person a timeline by which the problem must be handled. Ask for documentation or some kind of concrete proof that the problem has been taken care of. You don't have to be heavy handed, but you must take at least one concrete step. I've worked in too many situations where the boss would come down hard on someone who was committing the same problem over and over again but would never actually DO anything about it. If it needs 'writing up,' unless you actually do write it up, nothing will ever change. For the second direct report, file in your brain for the next time that you need to put your directions in writing. In most cases, that's all you'll have to do. Then ask your person to check in with you from time to time to determine progress.

YOUR Fault Workspace

Your boss stomps into your office and slaps down a sheaf of papers. He says, "This is a bunch of junk! This report has so many flaws I don't even know where to begin!" You were part of the tam that put together the report but you're pretty sure you own part was well and correctly done. Outline your conversation with the boss based on what you've learned about handling DPs. What are you going to say to Boss?

Coworker phones you with a panicky voice to say, "Please cone and help me with this presentation on our new product. I absolutely can't get it finished in time to the presentation at 9 AM tomorrow. Hellllllllp!" You know she's had this assignment for at least a week, and meanwhile, you have your own part of the presentation to fine tune. Outline your conversation with her based on what you've learned. What will you say to her?

Put your teacher ears on. Your 'favorite' student slides up to your desk late one afternoon. He says, "MS Teacher, I'm not going to be able to finish my part of the group report because Sam didn't finish his part and so I can't finish my part. Please give me an extra day!?!" Unfortunately, this is the third assignment this month that is in danger of not being completed by Favorite Student because, according to him, someone else hasn't done his share of the work. Outline your conversation with him based on what you've learned. What will you say to him?

Notes to Self:

Mental Games

One thing you absolutely do NOT want to do to try to deal with Difficult People is to try to outsmart them. Don't get into mental games with them. Difficult People make you think backwards...they get YOUR logic screwed up.

Difficult People are what is called 'loopers.' They refuse to solve a problem in a direct line, because they don't really see the need to solve the problem, or they don't even see a problem at all. Actually, they don't think they ever *have* a problem. They think it's *you*! They try to distract you by circling around and around in a conversation, circling back to something you said 10 minutes ago, recalling something someone not even with you said 10 days ago. They purposely try to get you off the subject so they can get control of the conversation and sidetrack you into giving them their own way. Eventually, you start to think *you're* the one who's nuts!

You- the boss, the team leader-call in a direct report/team member to discuss her constant backbiting of her colleagues, aloud and in public. It's gotten bad enough that morale in your department is suffering and the quality of work is also beginning to suffer. You start the conversation by going over the documentation you have gathered over the past month. You hear, "But, Boss, I never said that!" "Boss, but last year when Mary said..." "Well, you never say anything to John when he repeats..." "Why are you nailing me when Jerry is always...?" "When I talked to Sherry in Corporate Office last week she said..." "I've never gotten a bad evaluation..." "I'm always trying to do exactly what you want me to do..." "The people in the Finance Department are always talking about Joe because he can never...."

Do you get the picture? By now you're probably thinking something like, now why was it I wanted to see her????

What you *have* to do is to keep coming back to your documented episodes. You must say, "I don't know what Mary is saying." "I'm not here to talk about John." "I'm not 'nailing' you. I'm saying that this is the behavior I have seen." Keep to those old 'I messages': I see that on November 24th you said...... On December 2 you repeated......which was a piece of gossip from...." Go through your whole list regardless of the distracting comments and whines.

When you have gone through your list, make a specific statement to this person about what <u>behavior </u>you want to see from her in future. Just saying you want her to stop the trash talk won't work. You must outline specific things she must do, or in this case, not do, in order to keep herself out of trouble, or maybe even from getting fired. She doesn't care if her negative remarks hurt other people, but she will care if her negative remarks will get her fired.

You must also set a check in time for every so often. Go ahead and set an appointment for her to check in with you in, say, two weeks. If you need to, go another two weeks. These meetings probably will take you all of ten minutes and will eventually save you much hard feeling from your other direct reports.

Mental Games Workspace

Think about the last interaction you had with a DP in your office.

What kind of mental game(s) does she play that keep you from having a constructive relationship?
1. 2. 3.
How does this 'game' make you feel when dealing with her?
How do you typically respond to her games?
What's your plan for talking to her the next time you have an unpleasant interaction with her?
What episodes of gaming behavior can you document for her?
What can you do to keep her from looping on you?
What kinds of things can you say to her to keep her on track?

What specific behavior(s) do you want to see from her in the future?

How will you schedule check in times with her?

Notes to Self:

Policies

One thing you can do if you're the boss dealing with one or more difficult employees is to make sure you have both written and stated policies that apply to everyone.

And I truly mean, say the policy out loud in some kind of general meeting. We all know that some people never read the company handbook so there's a great reason for your DP to ignore company policies.

I learned a long time ago that treating people fairly doesn't necessarily mean treating everyone exactly the same. Different people have different needs, but it makes sense to have some policies that are exactly the same for everyone. For example, if you're in an elementary school and children come in the doors at 8AM, then every adult must be in the building at 7:45, no exception, no excuses. That's a safety matter, not a matter for interpretation or negotiation. If you're the supervisor in the Intensive Care Unit, personnel must be in the unit at all times, unless specifically relieved by someone who has signed in to take their place. Again, that could be a matter of life or death, so there's no slipping down to the canteen to grab a quick cup of coffee without telling anyone and getting someone to take your place. And in this instance the policy that states workers must be *in* the unit does NOT mean standing right outside the door chewing the fat, or slipping out on the balcony to grab a quick smoke.

You might also want to post written copies of appropriate policies in multiple places in your building/office. **Written in big bold lettering**. In some extreme color of ink. **Right beside all doors.**

Obviously, not all office/department policies are matters of life or death, but also obviously, someone high up in the organization thought they were important enough for the business to make them policies. That means that everyone in the organization adheres to them, whatever they are, or however silly they seem to some employees.

Now, we are all, as bosses, really good at following policies, but here's the hard part: *whenever you make an exception for one person, make sure you have specific criteria for that exception.* So, for example, your nurse employee dashes out of the ICU after grabbing her purse and car keys, leaving no one in her place. What do you do? She ran out because she just got a call that her 16 year old was in a car accident. That asks for an exception to the policy, given the circumstances. Your 4th grade teacher doesn't make it into the building till 8:30 leaving you scrounging to find coverage for her classroom. She got her 2 year old to daycare and then he got so sick she had to rush him back home to her husband. That asks for an exception. In both cases the employees never even thought about following the correct policy; they were operating purely on emotion.

There's no way you can have an 'exceptions to the policy' list, but you can set general parameters for exceptions to the rule:

1. Child's illness, serious enough to cause concern (be as clear as you can be here; you don't want people to be out with kids with the sniffles)
2. Spouse illness

3. Spouse or child accident causing injury
4. Employee illness severe enough to require a doctor
5. Employee accident causing injury

In most instances, whether or not the employee's behavior could cause a horrendous situation, there's not much other reason to be somewhere else rather than where you're supposed to be.

Policies Workspace

Do you know the policies in your office/building?
What are the policies that are NOT flexible? 1. 2. 3. 4. What are the policies that ARE flexible, as far as you know? 1. 2. 3. 4.
What are the penalties for not following standard policies in your office/building?
1. 2. 3. 4.
Do you feel that policies are enforced even handedly for everyone?
Not exactly the same for everyone because that is not necessarily fair?
Is there a particular policy you feel could be enforced more effectively?
If so, what policy is it?   How would you enforce it differently to make the policy more equitable for all?

Is there a policy you feel needs to be flexible that isn't presently flexible?

If so, what policy is it?

How would you change the policy to make it more flexible?

Is there a policy that you think is totally unnecessary?

If so, which policy is it?

Why do you think it is unnecessary?

Should it be replaced with a different policy?

If so, how would you word the replacement policy?

Is there a policy you wish existed in your building/office?

If so, what would be the policy? Draft it below.

Why do you think there should be a policy on this particular subject?

Notes to Self:

Stand Up!

Here's something you can easily do when you are faced with a Difficult Person.

Stand up!

Standing up communicates to this person, whether she is standing or not, that you mean business. You are communicating with your body. You are essentially saying, nonverbally, "I'm not here to fight with you. I'm not here to be taken advantage of. I'm not here to be run over by you. I'm here to be taken seriously."

Someone told me once long ago in my professional life that if you have a need to be liked more than a need to be taken seriously you need to find a job maybe with kindergartners. You have very little control over whether people like you or not; you have enormous control over whether people take you seriously.

If it's your boss who traps you at your desk to yell at you, get up and come around from behind the desk, calmly. You are not trying to threaten or intimidate her. Neither one of those attitudes works, because remember, this is all your fault anyway! But you can stand up and move to a window or a door or a framed certificate and then turn to face the boss. Show her you are listening but you are not going to crawl under the desk. You may have to count to 30 under your breath until she's through. When she is she may simply stalk out of your office, or you may be able to negotiate with her to do some problem solving of your own and then get back to her in a specified time. But either way, you have survived.

If you're the boss, this idea of standing up while you have the employee seated, preferably with a desk between you, is a long well-known tactic, but bosses are often reluctant to try it, because they would much rather be the nice guy than the boss. You may stand behind your desk or walk around it, or walk around the classroom, office, conference room while you employee remains seated. Again, you're not wanting to threaten or intimidate. You are wanting to say, take this situation seriously. But then, you must have a plan of steps that you want the employee to take, a time frame for the execution of the plan, and some kind of accountability activity for the employee to demonstrate compliance. The four key points for you as the boss:

1. Keep to the facts
2. Say out loud specific steps the employee is to take
3. Put the steps in writing when you get the chance and share them with the DP
4. Set a deadline by which these steps must be taken
5. Set an accountability activity for the employee at the end of the stipulated time frame.

Remember, if you don't follow up, you will not get the behavior you want.

Stand UP! Workspace

A DP you work with/work for/who works for you:

The characteristic(s) that make him difficult to work with:
1. 2. 3.

The behavior(s) you'd like to see from him:
1. 2. 3. 4.

The facts you have collected to document his difficult behavior(s):
1. 2. 3. 4.

Three steps you want him to take before your next interaction with him:
1. 2. 3.

How have you presented these steps to him?
How will you conduct your meeting with him? (Hint: how will you 'stand up' to him?) How have you written these steps? What's the format?

What's the deadline you've given him?
Why did you pick this deadline?

How will you know that he has completed these steps?
What behavior(s) will he exhibit in his general interactions with others? 　　1. 　　2. 　　3.

How will you monitor him during this process?

How will you follow through with him if he has not followed through himself?

Notes to Self:

Fight or Run Away?

Unfortunately for most of us who work for or with Difficult People, we are eventually going to lose our own temper after being yelled at for the umpteenth time, or having to redo a report for the umpteenth time, or having to do a useless task for the umpteenth time.

Or, if you're the long suffering type, you just eat the DP's words, and walk away with no reaction, that is, no overt reaction. You just give yourself ulcers or migraines by repeatedly sucking it up, when you know you should be doing something to counteract the barrage but you're afraid to or you're too stunned to.

If your boss is a DP who provokes a wish in people to yell back, first learn his pattern of losing his temper. Pay attention to what circumstances or times of day or month he's most likely to lose it at you (or anyone else) for seemingly no reason. Keep a kind of calendar for a month or two. You'll probably find that there's some kind of pattern to what sets him off. Once you learn the pattern you can more easily head off the worst of the attacks. And usually these episodes only last a couple of minutes. If you've done some of your own study, you'll know this and you'll also know not to return the verbiage in kind. Yelling back won't do anything but make you feel better for 30 seconds. The boss doesn't care at that moment whether you're right or wrong about the specific situation.

And remember that this behavior doesn't just mean yelling and screaming loudly. It also applies to people who do other mean little things to sabotage the office atmosphere or the quality of the work other people are doing. It could also mean that this DP just loves to get in your face and 'holler' quietly but just loud enough for everyone else around to know what's going on; that's how he gets his emotional gratification. You stand it as long as you can ant then you lose it yourself, either by yelling back or getting into the DP's face. Not a good idea! Or it could be the colleague who has his 15th meltdown for the year over a form he can't seem to get right. Or the one who has a crying fit about a spreadsheet she can't figure out.

The first thing to do—hard at first, I admit—is to do that old trick of silently counting to 10, or 20, or even 30 while he's ranting. That at least keeps your brain tied up long enough to keep you from lashing out yourself,, and finding yourself in the unemployment line. Then breathe, breathe, breathe. By this time the rant has probably run its course and you can move on to the second step. And for heaven's sake, even if you are just about to lose your cool, *don't* do it in front of other people! Think about that. Go somewhere where it's just you and the boss. Chances are you will make no headway anyway by saying, "Boss, it really bothers me when you yell at us for no reason." He's the boss.

The second thing to remember is to stick to the facts, no matter how hard that is for you at the moment. If you've done your homework, you can say something like, "OK, I understand your problem with the monthly finance report being perfect and in on time. How about if I go right now and check on the report with the finance officer and the data collection department and come back in 30 minutes or so to fill you in." you've done two constructive thing at the same time here: you've defused the yelling somewhat, and you've 'run away' by removing yourself from the temporarily volatile situation while at the same time acknowledging that the boss is the boss (a little ego boosting never hurts) and still being able to accomplish your goal of getting something done.

If you find you're getting nowhere and the rants are getting worse you need to document, even if it is your boss, and speak to someone in your human resources department.

If you're dealing with a coworker who is a yeller/screamer, that you *don't* have to put up with. The best thing to do here is to remove yourself from the immediate situation, even if it's aimed at you. Then come back in 10 minutes with a plan for solving the problem. Make sure the plan focuses on what the coworker is going to *do*, not how *you're* going to solve the problem. So if this coworker can't seem to ever make a spreadsheet come out right, that's probably what causes the major screaming and if she's always responsible for the spreadsheet, that's what causes the screaming. You could offer to teach her how to set up a template that she could use every month. Don't do the filling in yourself; that just means the whole job will devolve onto you. Don't set up the template yourself. Do offer to take 30 minutes to teach her how to set it up. And then maybe offer to check her figures the first couple of times she needs to do the spreadsheet. It's worth it to you not to have to put up with the screaming same time every month, or every day........

Fight or Run Away? Workspace

Think about your usual reaction to a bad situation. Are you the kind to stand and fight, or one to run?

Someone in your office whose behavior provokes you and/or your colleagues to want to retaliate in kind:

What is the behavior that most often provokes people almost beyond endurance

Do you find any observable pattern to this behavior?
If so, what is the pattern?

If you could respond in kind without any fear of repercussion, what would you love to do/say to him?

Your plan to handle him the next time he gets in your face:
Remember that Step 1 is to keep a kind of mental calendar for a couple of months to find the pattern to his outbreaks. What's the pattern?
Once you know the pattern, what can you do to head of his DP behavior, or at least lessen it?

Your Action Plan for interacting with him on the next project:
1.
2.
3.
4.
5.

What kind of response do you want from him the next time you interact with him?

Notes to Self:

SECTION 2:
SPECIFIC KINDS OF DIFFICULT PEOPLE

Absolute Control Freak

Difficult People want absolute control of every situation and they will do absolutely anything to get it. This mostly stems from the fact that they generally have a bad case of low self- esteem: they are afraid they are not as smart or as competent as everyone else they know. So they hide this fear in a cloud of controlling behavior.

So for example, the boss hands your team an important large report to do, puts a timeline on it and says something like, "Go for it." You and your colleagues get busy on the various parts of the report and you are sailing along smoothly...you think. A day into your work, the boss comes along and says, "I want to see what you have so far." He reads what you have, and moves on to the next of your team members with the same demand. Suddenly you hear that you're not doing at all what he wanted you to do! Surprise, surprise! He decides he wants you to backtrack and do this, this, and this with your various pieces of the report. OK, so you back up and redo. But guess what, he's back again in a day or so, wanting to see what you have. And, again, you each have to backtrack because you didn't get it right, *again*. So by the time he is finally satisfied with the report, you and your team members have probably done three or four different reports altogether and the version you did the first time through is the one he finally ends up accepting.

What you need to think about is that this boss is not a perfectionist. If he were a perfectionist he would have let you all complete one report and then picked at the pieces he though needed fixing. That you can mostly deal with once you know the form of his perfectionism. This boss is a control freak. He's not particularly concerned about the content you keep doing and redoing. He just wants you all to know that *he's* the boss and he can control everything you do, at least in the office.

Controlling behavior shows up in other circumstances, like the boss who requires a staff meeting every Monday morning from 8-10 AM, whether or not anyone else needs to be there. There could be absolutely nothing important that needs to be discussed, but the boss wants you there for the full time anyway.

Or the boss who refuses to see you or your colleagues on the spur of the moment when you have a problem. He keeps specific office hours and you must sign up for his attention. You could stand in his open door for 30 minutes and he would never see you.

There are a couple of things you can do with a severely controlling boss.

In the case of the report situation, before you even put pen to paper get the boss to tell you specifically what he wants, point by point if you can get it. That may be a little hard to do at first, but hang in there. You can say something like, "Boss, we can handle parts A. C, and E because they require pretty straightforward charts, but on parts B and D, what do you want us to be sure to include?" You are acknowledging that he is in control, but you are beginning to get your needs met too. You will probably still have to put up with some controlling behavior on the report, but you probably won't have to do five different versions, maybe just two. And when he comes around to tell you haven't got this version right, ask, "Can you clarify points 1, 3, and 5 before I restart them?" Again, you're acknowledging his control and giving him a little ego boost, which never hurts him or you.

In the case of a situation like the boss who holds useless meetings, bring some menial paperwork to do while you are listening. It would be nice if you could read a book or a report while he is droning on, but that would get you into deep hot water. However, if you are writing something down it looks a whole lot more industrious. Just be sure you are not doing anything that will keep you from paying attention with one ear, so you can make appropriate responses when needed.

Absolute Control Freak Workspace

A DP you work with who is a control freak:

How does he act that makes you think he's a control freak?

How does this behavior impact you and/or you work?

List three things you can do to help you survive his controlling behavior(s):
1.   2.   3.

What can you and your colleagues do together to work with him?
Remember that you are not trying to sabotage anyone or anyone's career: you and your colleagues can devise a plan that will mean success for everyone involved.   -   -   -   -   -

How would you like him to respond to you and/or your colleagues?

Is there anything else you can think of that will make the situation more bearable?

Notes to Self:

Bad Job!

Your boss gives you a task that you know has no chance of succeeding. Lots of bosses have pet projects or pet ideas or pet processes. Of course, most people have pet projects, feelings, and ideas but if it's your boss, you've got a problem. So she sends you off to do a job the department finance officer has already indicated is not financially feasible at this time. Boss doesn't seem to acknowledge this fact or even much care.

Forget arguing. Agree with the parts of the task you think, or know, will work, and then suggest some alternative ideas that you know *will* work. Be enthusiastic about the task as it is given to you, and then be equally enthusiastic about some other ideas that you know are proven. However, before you present your alternatives, take a little time to do your research or your thinking. You don't want to come across to the boss as just argumentative. So you could come back around and say, "Boss, it turns out we can't do the whole thing right now because of financial limitations but I *can* do parts 2, 3 and 6 for no additional cost and have that much on your desk by Thursday. Then maybe we can work out the financing for parts 1, 4, and 5, and get the whole project completed." You've defused what could have been a bad confrontation, while still letting the boss know you're working on the task she assigned you just as she assigned it.

But what happens when your boss gives you an awful task that you know won't work, and she won't listen to any of the suggestions you and/or your colleagues have offered as more successful alternatives?

The best thing to do here is get it in writing. If possible get the boss to put it in writing, but if she won't *you* put it in writing and get the boss to sign off on it. You can tell her you're making sure you understand the task and the steps you need to take to successfully complete the task, which is true, but you will also have some protection when the thing falls in.

Bad Job! Workspace

What's an example of a task you've been given in the past that was barely, or not at all, workable?

What was the outcome of that task?

List three things you can do to make sure you're as successful as possible the next time you're handed a similar task:
1. 2. 3.

What can you say to the boss the next time you are faced with a similar task?

How will you hold the boss 'accountable' when faced with a similar bad task?

Notes to Self:

Boasters

Then there's the coworker who is the local know-it-all, who just loves to show you and everyone else how intelligent he really is, how much he knows about everything in the world. And he most often confesses this 'fact' in staff meetings or company meetings so *everyone* can know how wonderful he is. He also loves to put people down by boasting about how easy the job was, when you were wiping your brow just barely getting your part of the project done. He expounds on how he got his part of the job done in half the time everyone else did, when you were all grateful just to finish before the deadline. Or how he sold twice the products as his quota called for and you didn't.....

You can do two things here to help you survive with this lovely person.

The first thing you need to remember is that taking it all with a grain of salt is always a good antidote to chest thumpers. Acknowledge your coworker's expertise, let it go, and know you did a good job, and that this coworker is always going to go for the backhanded put down of you and everyone else.

Second, make sure you've done your homework on the situation at hand, so you can contradict him if you need to. You don't have to be obnoxious about it, no matter how badly you want to be, but do point out – gently – an incorrect fact or inconsistency in information he gives out before things go sideways. Don't say out loud, especially not in a public meeting, "You dummy, we actually did that two years ago!" Or, "Check the rule book, idiot, because I think it actually says_____!" If he's so full of himself that he's claiming all knowledge, attack his facts, not him. But do it gently and make sure you're right.

Boasters Workspace

A boaster in your office/department:
What does he boast about?

Does he boast about a real area of expertise?
If so, what?

How does his boasting impact your ability to do your job?

What's your plan for the next time you interact with him, especially if you are assigned a common task?

What will you say to him?

What will you do?

How will you monitor the situation?

Notes to Self:

Bossy Explosions

If your DP is a boss who is one of those people who goes along smoothly for a while and then all of a sudden just explodes for no reason you can fathom, your best bet is to just listen. Listen, listen, listen! This is the boss you don't have any problems with, until...... The explosions are only infrequent and don't usually last long, otherwise he's a pretty good fellow to work for.

Even if you're the one being exploded on, just hold on. Everyone around you has been in the same situation and knows exactly what you're going through. Wait him out. Nothing you can do or say will calm him down; you can only know he will eventually run out of steam. However, if the explosion doesn't seem to be coming to an end any time soon you can say something like, "Boss/Jane/Don, I'll come back and talk to you in ten minutes or so." Say it pleasantly. Then walk out of the space where you're catching so much grief. No, this isn't rude. It's a matter of self-preservation. But be sure you're back in the ring in ten minutes so your credibility doesn't suffer. Interestingly enough, the exploder probably won't even register any insult on your part because he's still in 'explode mode.'

Bossy Explosions Workspace

A typical 'bossy' explosion looks like:

How often do these explosions happen?

Is there a particular occurrence that causes an explosion?

How have you reacted to an explosion in the past?

What's your plan for responding to an explosion the next time?
Think through carefully: What will you say?   How will you behave?

What will you do or say *differently* from how you used to respond?

Notes to Self:

Bully Bosses

You know who they are. They may be the screamers or they may just nail you quietly when you least expect it. These are the bosses who say things like, "I'm going to write you up if you don't get me those figures by 3 PM." Or, "You're not pulling your weight around here, you'd better show me something soon on this project!" Or, "I have no intention of giving you any extra time on this assignment because you shouldn't need it." Or, "I think I'll give this assignment to _____ because I don't think you can handle it." Bullies aren't necessarily loud, they really just like to mess with your head. However, they are smart enough not to cross the line by flat out calling you stupid, or an imbecile.

Psychiatrists say a bully cannot exist without at least one victim. Your business is to not become the handiest victim. If your boss really is a bully, and you really have become the victim, you have a real interest in *not* losing your job because of your own responses to the boss.

If the bully has you tied up in ropes about a project and is wearing you down, one thing you can do is to ask for a time to explain to the boss where you are in the project. A technique that will work here is to ask for a specific amount of time to explain where you are and what you are doing. Say, " I'd like to have ten (five, fifteen) minutes of your time so I can go over where I am on each step of the project." Bring notes, schedules, charts, dashboards, spreadsheets. This keeps the focus on the project and gets it out of the personality realm. This usually works because it sidetracks the bully boss into thinking about something else besides how stupid you are. It especially works if you throw in the point that you are recasting a couple of steps based on what the boss has suggested (suggested, really????).

Now, if you find yourself in the barrel all the time, and nothing you try has worked, unfortunately, the best thing to do here is to get out on the QT and begin looking for another job before you are completely emotionally wiped out.

Bully Bosses Workspace

Kind(s) of bullying your boss indulges in?

How have you and/or your colleagues reacted in the past?

On the emotional side, how does this bullying make you feel?

So why do you allow this behavior to continue?
Be honest with yourself here. Look inside yourself to think about how you respond to this behavior and why you think you respond as you do.

What's your plan for handling the bullying the next time you're in the barrel?

Think through carefully, what will you bring to your next meeting with the bully?

Notes?

Schedules?

Charts?

Dashboards?

Spreadsheets?

Time frame?

Suggestions you could offer?

Notes to Self:

Chewing the Fat

Is your partner on a project spending more time chewing the fat around the coffee machine and checking up on everyone's social life than working on your project, which, of course, is due to be completed in two days? He is good at what he does, and his harmless fat-chewing doesn't cause any real problems. Otherwise, he gets his tasks completed well and mostly on time. So this particular problem is mainly one of aggravation – to you and your coworkers, not him.

Some people are just naturally more social butterfly than worker bee. If this is your partner there are a couple of things you can do. Thank goodness this coworker is not as hard to get back on track as some other DPs.

First, clearly list the pieces of the project you will be responsible for and put dates to every step you will complete.

Then help your coworker by doing the same kind of thing for him, and don't leave out the dates! You may think you're doing extra work here, but it pays to also remember whose fanny will be on the line if the project doesn't get completed correctly and on time.

Chewing the Fat Workspace

Where does your coworker hang out most to chit chat?

How have you responded to her in the past?

How does her chatty behavior impact you and the way you do your job?

What's your plan for dealing with her chattiness the next time the two of you are handling an assignment together?

How will you monitor her parts of the project?

What do you want her end of the project to look like?

Notes to Self:

Cliques

In most offices, people tend to hang around with people they like and with whom they have similar interests. Unfortunately, that means that sometimes cliques form within the office. You can generally eventually figure out who's in which clique by which people you see together most of the time. There is always a 'ringleader' in a clique, and several followers. Most of the time these cliques are harmless. They are folks who play golf, folks who like going to the local pub on Fridays, folks who are interested in a certain aspect of the office's tasks, folks who have teenagers giving them trouble. If there's a clique that really begins to cause problems in the office, that can take a couple of aspects: morale in the office is being sabotaged; assignments are not getting done on time or correctly.

Occasionally, when a clique starts to turn the atmosphere in the office sour, you need to find the ringleader first. That takes time and patience: just be aware of and listen in on conversations, watch seating patterns in meetings, check out which people gather in whose office.

An easy step to take once you know who's in charge of the clique is to invest some time in getting the ringleader on your side. You have a couple of good options here: you can occasionally give him a really good assignment; you can ask him to plan a special meeting or other activity. Those kinds of things are innately empowering to the person who's been asked. Your main purpose here is to sort of mentor, not sanction.

If you turn your attention to the members of the clique themselves you can do a couple of things. If it has gotten out of control, and you're the boss, you can reassign clique members to different teams. Or you can give them different hours from one another. And if worse comes to worst, and you can, you can transfer some of them out of your office completely. Case closed!

On the other hand, if you've got a recognizable clique, but they are doing a good job and get along well with one another, give them specialized assignments that play to their group strength. In this way, as long as they keep working above average you can call them an 'official' clique.

And there's nothing saying that if you are one of the clique's colleagues you can't join them, or work alongside them, or suggest to the boss that she can change assignments, or 'put a bug in her ear' about what would make the clique work better in the office. After all, you have a vested interest in their working well with others, even if you're on the outside looking in.

And anyway, you have your own clique, don't you?

<u>Cliques Workspace</u>

What is/are the cliques in your office?
Be honest here. You know there's at least one! Designate each clique by its common 'theme.' 1. 2. 3.

Who is the ringleader in each clique, as far as you can determine?
1. 2. 3.

How does each clique affect the atmosphere in the office?
1.   2.   3.

How do you work with each clique?

Is there a clique you need to work around?
If so, what's your plan for working around it? Step 1:   Step 2:   Step 3:

Do you have your own clique?

Again, be honest here. How would you describe your clique (your group of friends)?

What's the major strength of your clique?

Who's the 'boss' in your clique?

How does your clique work together best?

If you could identify a weakness in your clique, what would it be?

How could you address this weakness, by yourself or with some others?

Look at your clique carefully. How do you all together contribute to the wellbeing of your office as a whole?

Now go back and look at the cliques you first identified. If you were the BIG Boss, how would you work with each clique to make it more effective and/or less hostile to the atmosphere in the office? And think positive!

1.

2.

3.

Notes to Self:

Criticism, Criticism

What if your DP is your boss or your team leader, who never seems to have anything good to say about you and can always find something to criticize you for in a heartbeat? Eventually you realize she is woefully lacking in people management skills. Actually, she doesn't manage people well at all. It's probably not just *you* who suffers from her criticisms.

There are a couple of things you can do here when you've had enough. The best thing for you to do is counter her criticism with facts. What you say is something like, "I hear you, and what I did is format this finance report exactly like you had me do with the last one. I'll get you my notes on that one if you want me to." Then you leave without editorializing any more. Don't say anything else. Don't make excuses. Don't apologize. Don't be confrontational. But do be sure to bring back your notes to go over them with her as soon as possible if she wants to see them.

A second alternative if you perhaps have not done exactly this kind of task before and you're being criticized, you can say, "May I make an appointment to sit down with you and make some notes or come up with an outline to follow every time I do this _____ report in the future?" Again, don't be confrontational, don't make excuses. You're looking for information from the boss that will make her criticism unnecessary. If you follow her orders exactly, and you've got them written down from her own mouth, you should be in good shape if she chooses to criticize you again; just pull out your notes.....

But what about the team leader who is actually just slightly short of being verbally abusive to you and/or your colleagues? You think you can do nothing about this. Ah, but you can! What you need to know first, though, is that this kind of person will never change, unless you stand up him, in a positive way. She won't respect you as long as you give in and give her her own way at every turn, just to try to avoid the verbal abuse. The sad truth is that this DP is really a coward who wants her own way but she really doesn't want to deal with anyone who will stand up to her, stand toe to toe, or face to face, exactly because she *is* a coward.

Something you can say to a person like this is, "I know you said _____, but I don't think you realize that you've put me in a bad position here. Did you mean to say_____?" This way you're not trying to outmaneuver your DP, which won't work anyway because she is an excellent manipulator. But you are making an appeal to her sense of fairness, which, admittedly may be buried very deep, if there at all. And as soon as you say anything-calmly-chances are this DP will back down at least one notch very quickly. The key is to keep yourself low key in your responses to her.

Criticism, Criticism Workspace

Someone in your office who criticizes more than you think is normal?

What form(s) does his criticism take most often?

How do you and your coworkers normally respond to his criticisms?

How does his criticism impact your working relationship with him?

What's your plan for dealing with his criticism the next time you're the victim?
If you're the victim? What will you do?   What will you say?   If someone else is the victim? What will you do?   What will you say?

How do you want the criticizer to interact with you and your colleagues in the future?

What will this behavior look like?

Notes to Self:

Hard Headed

Your boss is so hardheaded that no one can argue with him once his mind is made up, even if you and your colleagues know he's got it wrong! And, no, that's not the beginning of a bad joke. And to make matters worse, his information is not the right information. His mind was made up before he even got the right information.

What you can do here is use facts to try to convince him that he might want to take a different tack than the one he is so stubbornly hanging onto. Take a few minutes, or a couple of hours, if you have to, to find some research on the subject, find some articles that pose different, more correct possibilities. Highlight the key points you think should be made and hand it to your boss. Don't editorialize. Don't offer any other points. Just tell him he might want to check out some additional information you've found before he plugs ahead with his (wrong) information. The point here is that you are trying to help, not trying to undercut him or correct him or insult his intelligence.

If your boss is so hardheaded that you can't make any headway with him on much of anything at any time, get some of your colleagues together and come up with a workable plan that your boss will have a hard time arguing against. Make sure your boss knows you've talked to a number of different people, again a form of research, and you all like this substitute idea a lot and that it's based on a particular research or a proven technique. Those kinds of facts are hard to argue with.

One thing you might also want to keep in mind is the speed with which you try to help your boss out of a bad situation. Think about this: it doesn't make any of you and your colleagues look particularly talented or on point if your boss stands up in a big meeting and spouts out a very bad idea that you knew about in advance. Think about your help as a possible matter of self-preservation and go for it!

Let's turn the table a minute. Suppose you're the boss and your local hard head reports to you. And she often gets herself in over her head on assignments you've given her (she doesn't want to disappoint you or upset you by telling you she's going to do it her way anyway).

Don't wait to let her fall flat on her face more than a couple of times if she's worth saving. As soon as you see she's having difficulty, sit her down and ask her if she has any questions about the assignment you've given her. For this type of person your best recourse is to write out the steps of the assignment for her, or dictate them to her, and go over them carefully with her as you talk.

Hard Headed Workspace

Someone in your office who's a hard head:
Think about a couple of past instances in which he was hard headed:
1.   2.
How did these instances impact the atmosphere or the tasks you and your colleagues were working on?
What's your plan for interacting with him the next time you come up against hard headed behavior?
1.   2.   3.   4.   5.
What can you do/say to help him out of a bad public situation?
1.   2.   3.

Notes to Self:

I Just Can't Seem to Get There On Time!

Your DP is really a good worker, but can't seem to get anywhere on time, or to any meeting on time. So your whole office or department is held captive in a meeting room waiting till he shows up so the meeting can start. You wonder if you should have brought your knitting!

The best thing to do is start without him! You honor the people who have shown up on time by starting the meeting on time.

If you are in charge of the meeting, when he finally makes it into the room, keep right on with your topic; don't say anything snarky, don't give him the evil eye, don't waste any more time on him. After being late to a few, or several, meetings, he will realize he has missed critical information each time he's been late. He'll get the message. If you're not the one in charge, you can gently prod the person who is leading the meeting that you have an important meeting scheduled at _____ o'clock and the boss has a vested interest in your being at that meeting. It shouldn't take too many meetings to convince the person in charge that time is valuable to everyone, not just the late comer.

But what if it's your boss who's the procrastinator, chronically late for everything (translate: lazy, spineless, inefficient) one thing you can do is to volunteer to do any legwork or research a project needs to get it started. Yes, this may mean extra work for you, but consider what might happen to you and your coworkers if your boss gets fired for inefficiency. Who's next on the firing line?

I Just Can't Seem to Get There on Time Workspace

Someone in your office who has a problem with being on time:

How does this tardiness impact you and your colleagues?

Your plan to deal with tardiness if the offender is a coworker:

1.

2.

3.

Your plan to deal with tardiness if the offender is your boss:

1.

2.

3.

Notes to Self:

I Know It ALL!

We all have these folks in our lives, both personal and professional. You know the ones. They can one-up you with anything and in any situation. He could be your boss or your colleague. He can always tell you better than you can tell him. He *always* has the right answer, whether it's the right answer or not..... Think Sheldon on "The Big Bang Theory."

You'd think he had Ph.D.s in everything from Biology to Chemistry to Accounting to Food Services. Because he can always tell you where you went wrong with *your* plan or your piece of a larger task. Or how you could have done it better. Or how you really should have tackled it from a different perspective. Or why your idea won't work, and his is better.

Or, worse, he slides into the boss's office to inform her about what's wrong with your report and then the boss appears at your door!

This one turns out to be easy.

First, don't argue. Don't expect to change his mind with all your carefully researched information. It won't make any difference even if you pull out reams of published research. This is a person who will fault the research!

Then just tap into all the expertise he has for real. Use his knowledge of certain subjects to your own advantage when you need it. Pick his brain for all he's worth when you need to. This serves two purposes: you not only get the advantage of someone else's knowledge and perspective, you stroke his ego, which isn't a bad thing!

I Know It ALL! Workspace

Someone in your office who knows everything about everything:

How does this behavior generally impact you and your colleagues?

Does this behavior negatively affect the atmosphere in your office?
If yes, describe:

What's your plan for dealing with him the next time you have a shared task?
1.   2.   3.   4.

How would you like him to respond to you in the future?

Think: what strengths and talents doe this DP really have that you can access?
Be honest....

Notes to Self:

I *Look* Good But.....

Now you're faced with the coworker who looks *really* good at what she does. She shuffles paper really well. But eventually you figure out she's really doing NOTHING. She's also probably the classic clock watcher; she can't wait to shuffle paper for the last time each day. Confronting her won't get you very far because she always has a million and one reasons for doing things the way she does (doesn't do) them.

Where you need to start with her is to look at your own part of an assignment to make sure you've absolutely done your part. If you're sure you're in the clear, the best, simplest thing to do is just ask your coworker what's wrong. How come her part of the project is not getting done? Just listen.... If you listen carefully enough you might have your own aha! moment about what's really at the bottom of her problem. That's the beginning of the process of getting her on track.

You could ask some very pointed but nonthreatening questions like, "What's the problem you're having with getting that resources chart done?" Or, "Can you help me understand why these dashboard numbers are missing/wrong?" Or, "What can I help you do to get this set of numbers to make sense?" Asking these kinds of pointed questions will get you a whole lot farther down the road than just ranting about why nothing ever gets done around here.

So what do you do with the coworker (otherwise known as 'the weasel'), who is very adept at weaseling out of everything and you have just now figured out that that's what she's been doing for a long time? Actually, you've just figured out that you're the one who is ending up doing the job most of the time. These are the whiners and the 'poor pitiful Pearls' of the world. She begs you to help her finish almost every job. She volunteers to the boss that she's not the best person for this project, but you are. She tells everyone else that she's already snowed under and so someone else will have to help her get the job done if you all don't want to come under the fish eye.

Once you have figured out that you're the patsy, pull that old drug awareness training slogan to the front of your brain: Just Say No! If your plate is already full you don't even need a reason to turn down someone's request for a favor, especially if you've done it time and time again already. If saying No is hard for you, you can be appropriately sad for her by saying, "Wish I could help, but I already have_____ that I need to finish by deadline myself. However, if I have any extra time I will certainly be glad to help you." You, of course, know that you will not have any spare time. Eventually, "Pearl" will get the hint.

I *LOOK* Good But..... Workspace

Someone in your office whom you suspect of 'looking good':

How does his 'looking good' behavior impact you?

What does his 'looking good' behavior look like?

How would you like this behavior to change?

What's your plan for dealing with him the next time you're impacted with this behavior?
1.
2.
3.
4.

What steps will you take to monitor his relearning process?
What kinds of questions will you ask him to help you finish a task?
1.
2.
3.

Is there a weasel in your office?

If you're her patsy, how will you deal with her to keep from being an eternal patsy?
1.
2.
3.

Notes to Self:

Just Following Orders

You have a direct report who is a perfectionist who insists upon 'following the rules' at all times, 'following company policy', 'following the regulations', at all times and in all circumstances, even when the situation calls for some flexibility. And he just loves to tell you how you have loused up the situation by *not* following the rules. He's the person who snidely remarks, "Well, if you had just looked at page 47, section C3 in the rulebook...." Or, "This would never have happened if we had used Regulation A, # 4....."

What you can do here is to say right up front, before you assign a project, that this particular project will *require* people to use their own judgment on different sections. Then define the kind of judgment calls you're thinking about. Then define the range of what these actions can be. Once these ideas are spelled out, the perfectionist will feel more comfortable about being 'allowed' to flex the rules.

Also, make sure you're familiar enough with the particular rule book that you can speak to whichever of the rules or policies she's referring to. If you're not familiar with it, go find it and look up the pertinent information before you talk to her again.

For example, you may give some latitude on how the budget gets spent for the project. As long as people back up their expenditures they may use their own insights on where to spend the money. Or you may allow time to flex. The project must be completed by a specific date but you will let people choose how they will spend their time completing it, whether they work on it regularly, periodically, or all at the last minute, as long as it's completed on time and well.

If the 'orders' person is your boss, just reverse the information you give your direct report. In other words, when you receive an assignment from her, before you do anything else ask, "Boss, what kind of independent judgment calls can we make on our own on this assignment?" "Is there any extra latitude we can use on the budget? The time frame? The kinds of research we use?" "Do you want us to pay particular attention to the _____ section in the company manual?" "Do you want us to check in with you periodically?" You get the picture. The more you get spelled out from this kind of person, the better off you'll be.

And remember that the more you spell out for everyone assigned to the same task, the smaller the opportunity for any kinds of mistakes.

Just Following Orders Workspace

A perfectionist who depends on 'orders' to make himself feel respected?

Does she have a particular 'orders' obsession?
That is: rule book? Company manual? What the boss says at all times? What the boss writes all the time? Corporation policy notebook? Rules posted outside the door?

How does her behavior impact how you do your job?

What's your plan for interacting with her the next time you think you might be conflicting with her 'orders'?
For example, what kinds of information will you give her before she starts an assignment?   If she's your boss, what kinds of clarifying questions will you ask?

Notes to Self:

Liar, Liar

What if your Difficult Person is a chronic liar? These are the people who would, as my mother says, lie when the truth would fit better.

Her part of the report is all ready, according to her, but for one thing, and you happen to know it's not even started. She is late for the third time this week because of car trouble. She has to leave early for the second time this week because she has a sick child. She says something like, "Well, I don't know why he's not here; I talked to him last night and he said he'd be here....." You can put up with some fibs as long as they are small enough, but telling falsehoods, or stretching the truth even, can turn office morale sour in a hurry. Or everyone could go down with the liar if she tells one too many! Everyone knows where the truth lies with this person and it's shaky at best.

In this case your only option is to go straight for the facts. Gather up your factual information before you confront her. Don't argue; don't get sucked into a debate. Just give her the facts. You don't need to pass judgment on her; sooner or later someone in a higher position of authority will get tired of the untruths and have a whole other conversation with her. If this person reports to you, you might want to do a little sleuthing if the lying gets to be so habitual. It's not hard to call a daycare center and check on children or talk to a coworker who happens to know what the real story is. You don't want to end up playing Sherlock Holmes, but in your own best interest you might do a little checking for some background information.

But what about the person who doesn't exactly lie, but is overly fond of making himself look good by telling half-truths or omitting important pieces of information. A great example here is the fellow who considers himself the expert on designing web pages, so when you request a few lessons he conveniently leaves one step out so your web page ends up a mess. Or the person who wants control of the budget allocation process and only tells you *most* of the steps but not all of them so he can keep the power to himself, and, if he's lucky, make you look stupid at the same time!

Again, don't jump. Get your facts together, present them to your problem person, and you've made your point. If your person has a habit of telling half-truths and making omissions in public meetings, just do the same thing: point out the facts of the case in a quiet, non-judgmental manner and your point is well made.

Liar, Liar Workspace

Someone in your office who seems not overly fond of the truth:

What kinds of things does he shade the truth about?

Does his problem with the truth impact the morale of the office?
If so, how?

Does his problem with the truth impact the quality of the assignments he shares with other coworkers?
If so, how?

What's your plan for interacting with him the next time you know he's not telling the truth?

What's your plan for dealing with him if his particular brand of 'fudging' continues after you have had a conversation with him?
This might be hard, but the situation might come to a confrontation eventually. What will you do?   What will you say?

What do you think you would do if this behavior occurs in an important public meeting?

Notes to Self:

Nitpickers

Nitpickers are hard to work for, hard to work with, and hard to supervise, because they can never seem to get to the end of a task; they keep finding little things that need to be changed in one way or another, or corrected, or added, or deleted, or moved....... Well, you get the picture. Usually nitpickers are as hard on themselves as they are on anyone else. A large part of their problem is that their self-esteem is pretty low and they feel that they themselves are not very creative. So they need to find fault wherever they can, with themselves or whoever else happens to be handy, to deflect away from what they perceive as their own lack of creativity.

What if it's your boss who's the nitpicker? A good idea here is to recruit him! You can ask him to double check your figures for a report, edit a section of the report, make sure charts are in the right places. That redirects his energy to something that he has control over and gets his nitpicking onto something important. If he's the type of boss who only wants *his* ideas out there and forget about anyone else's, what you need to do is appeal to his own self-interest or self-preservation. Show him how your idea moves *him* forward. Then he's more likely to trust your idea.

A second thing you can do with your boss is to ask him if it's OK to divide up the task. Generally, bosses don't care how something is done as long as *they* look good, so if the boss agrees to this tack, recruit some colleagues to help with some of the less important, easier parts of the task. That way you're not monopolizing *their* time, or adding to their work overmuch, and, as long as you keep the biggest chunk of the operation for yourself and double check your colleagues' pieces, your task should end up completed on time and in great shape.

There are a couple of things you can do if your nitpicker reports to you. She's the person who does a report over and over because she finds some minor flaw in it each time she rereads it, so it takes forever to get completed. What you have to do here is introduce her to reality, gently, as hard as that may seem. Before you assign her to do something, lay out ground rules you have already decided on. Put a time frame to the report and stick to it, whether the report is perfect or not. Give it a specific budget if you need to and, since you approve expenditures, you can cut off the project if it goes over budget. Chances are, at least one time, you will find yourself cutting off the project; nitpickers can run over time and budget quickly since they keep finding things they need to fix. But is shouldn't take more than once.

Another thing you can do with nitpickers, or perfectionists for that matter, is to help them with a major task by teaching t hem how to 'chunk' the task. Chunking is a technique used frequently by teachers to help their students with a large or difficult assignment. Help your nitpicker think through what needs to be done to complete the task. Then go through the information you've got and break up what needs to be done into smaller, similar, related tasks (chunks), by looking at all the little chores that could be lumped together. Check to make sure these tasks are in manageable chunks. You can also assign responsibilities into smaller sections if more than one person is working on the task. What happens here is that the nitpicker will get a sense of satisfaction from completing each section of the work, and then the final product ends up being done well.

Nitpickers Workspace

Someone in your office who's a nitpicker:

What kinds of things cause her to nitpick most frequently?

How does her nitpicking most impact your ability to complete a task?

If the nitpicker is your boss, what steps will you take to control her nitpicking during your next assignment?

1.

2.

3.

4.

If the nitpicker reports to you, what steps will you take to control the nitpicking the next time you assign her a task?
1.
2.
3.
4.
5.
This one may need a long term plan. What are a few ideas you have to head off any kind of emotional or professional melt down your nitpicker might have?
1.
2.
3.
4.
How will you monitor the nitpicking behavior over time?

Notes to Self:

Oh, My, Oh, My, Oh Sigh......

Difficult people are not always obviously angry or obnoxious or cruel. Sometimes people are difficult for a whole different reason. They are perpetual victims. They don't come across as overtly difficult until you begin to realize over time that Joan seems to provoke other people in the office to put her down. She sends out these 'Poor Pitiful Pearl' vibes that end up causing people to use her or hurt her.

What she does is act helpless in the face of a large or difficult task. Remember = the movie, 'The Fly,' when the fly is shrinking and he's screaming, "Help meeeeeee." Only with her these messages are non- verbal. She just looks at you pitifully. Or she flops down in the chair across from you and slaps a bunch of papers down on your desk and whines something like, "I'm confused...." This is your perpetual victim.

She has a habit of forgetting important dates or deadlines or appointments or meeting times and places. She's just asking to be stomped on. And she gets what she's asking for: a calling down from the boss, a letter of reprimand in her personnel file; a refusal of some people in the office to work with her anymore; snickers behind her back or to her front. She bears all insults with equanimity.

She really is very often used by other people to do tasks they don't want to do or see people they don't want to deal with. She very rarely stands up to her oppressors. She doesn't even make it an even match. She just carries on being helpless and hopeless. You could really call her a masochist if you thought about it long enough.

She does excellent work when you can get her on track, but it seems to take some real doing on your part. This is a person who is going to be around the office for a long time, because some other colleagues will stand up for her every time she screws up. Why? She does their dirty work and never complains! Oh, she might whine a lot about it but do you notice she never really asks for any concrete help? When she finally gets around to it, what she does is good, or good enough to keep her employed.

This is not a person who will get to be the boss very often, so that's not a problem you will probably ever have. However, if this *is* your boss, the smartest thing for you to do is simply listen to her. You can't fight her battles for her, since you don't have her authority. Someone higher up will eventually figure out this picture and handle it from a different perspective. Not your problem!

If this is a colleague, you can help her out by not letting her get to the whining stage. Cut her off if she's in your office being pitiful. Allot her a certain amount of time to finish crying. Tell her when she comes in, "I've got 10 minutes before my next meeting/my next appointment/I need to go to James's office." Then stick to it. Gently show her out your door at the end of your time limit. She'll go quietly because, remember, she loves being put upon.

If she's a direct report, give her written timelines for any work to be accomplished. Send her e mail reminders of meetings or appointments. Those can be programmed on a telephone or a computer, so it's not much of an effort on your part. And, here's the tricky part: if she's not working up to your expectations, *don't* listen to her colleagues defending her or taking her side. They may feel sorry for her, but they also want to use her skills and she wants them to abuse her time and efforts. Keep documentation of what you've done to try to help her, and if her work doesn't improve, take it to the next level.

Oh, My, Oh, My, Oh Sigh...... Workspace

Who is the "Poor Pitiful Pearl" in your office?

What does her pitiful behavior look like?

How does her behavior impact your ability to do your work well?

How does her behavior impact the emotional atmosphere of your office?

How do her colleagues generally react to her when interacting with her on a project?

What's your plan for dealing with her the next time she plops down forlornly in front of you?

What will you do?

What will you say to her?

How will you monitor her progress on meeting task goals?

1.

2.

3.

4.

Notes to Self:

Passive-Aggressives

Some difficult people are known to psychiatric literature as 'passive-aggressive.' They are really hard to spot and it may take you a long time before you say to yourself, "Hey, wait a minute...." Unfortunately they are very multi-faceted at being passive-aggressive, and you will have to recognize their pattern of behavior before you can learn to deal with them. These folks can really subvert a whole organization if you don't tackle them early on.

Passive-aggressiveness means that, among other problems, these folks are very good at making promises to get things done, but then somehow never seem to get things finished, or even get them started. They can, and do, lie frequently to everyone. They suck up to you for your help or opinion and then turn right around and badmouth you to your other coworkers; talk about a hypocrite! These people often talk in vague or uncertain terms about any assignment, because they are hoping someone will mistake their muddy language for insecurity and therefore decide to do most of the work for them. These are the original two-faced people: pitiful on one face, and out loud nasty on the other. There are a few ideas of what works with these people, however.

First, if your P-A is a coworker and you've both been assigned to the same project, write out a clear step-by-step calendar of each due date for each stage of the project. Even if you're not in charge of the project you can tell your co-worker that you need the list for your own benefit, to keep things straight in your own head. If you've been given specific instructions by the boss, rewrite them into one-syllable words as much as possible. Then periodically, check in with (check up on?) her just to make sure she's keeping up with your calendar. The main idea for you here is to keep her on track. You aren't her boss and you most probably aren't a psychiatrist, and you surely don't have time to get to the bottom of her problems, and you can't change her attitude, but you can certainly track and maybe change her behavior. And at least, you'll keep yourself out of trouble with the boss.

If you P-A is a coworker with whom you must deal periodically but not regularly, but you still need information or other data from him, you can still work with him relatively successfully if you do something similar. If your P-A is, for example, your company or department's Finance Officer and you need statistics from him, talk to him in one-syllable words. Ask questions that require only one or two words. In other words, keep your interactions with this person as simple as possible. You might also want to put your requests in writing; bulleted lists with a fill in the blank section work really well here. This advice is not meant to be insulting to anyone. It most often helps everyone involved if directions are kept as clear and simple as possible.

What happens if your passive-aggressive is your boss and he has given you and/or your department a vague, unclear assignment to complete in a very fast turnaround time? Get a clue: this probably means there is something inherently wrong with the project and the boss is sloughing off the responsibility to you, so that when the whole thing blows up in your face, you are set to take the fall.

The best thing to do here is to say right out loud that you are concerned about this project getting to a successful conclusion, and asking everyone in your department for some possible alternatives to solving the problems innate to the project. If you approach this right, you won't sound like *you're* whining. You can get some ideas down on paper and get your coworkers on board with some possibilities. This way your boss knows that *you* know what's going on, but you haven't been the least bit confrontational, and even if the project flops, you've been proactive in getting problems out there first. Remember, you're not trying to get around the boss, or make her look bad. What you *are* doing is probably saving a number of people from getting bogged down in a messy project and then not being able to do it well. Guess who comes out looking bad in that case? Think positively about what you are doing for all participants.

Passive-Aggressives Workspace

Someone in your office whom you suspect is a passive-aggressive:

Three examples of his passive aggressive behavior:
1.   2.   3.

How do you normally respond to his behavior?

How would you like to see his behavior change:
List two or three specific distracting behaviors that you would like to see change:

What's your plan for dealing with him the next time you must share a task with him?
1.   2.   3.

What's your plan for responding to him if he's your boss and he gives you a muddled assignment?

1.

2.

3.

4.

How will you monitor his behavior when you are working on a task with him?

1.

2.

3.

Notes to Self:

Rumor Mongers

Beyond the snoop/tattletale is the real rumor monger, the one who not only snoops and then tells, but the one who goes too far in spreading tales that don't even have the facts straight. She spreads half-truths around liberally. An old mentor of mine always said, "Perception is reality." If the perception that morale is going bad starts spreading around the office because someone's tale-telling is starting to interfere with how people do their jobs, you're in trouble. If someone in the office gets wind that a rumor has started about him that is not true, you're in trouble. If a half-false rumor gets to your boss, especially if it's about him, you're in trouble. This is a really unpleasant situation to confront but it needs to be tackled, whether you're a coworker or the boss.

So...if you know who the rumor monger is, sit her down in your office or cubby and ask her to walk you through the 'facts' of the story. Get her version of events. Then correct each false statement with the correct information you have already gathered. Do it one fact by one fact. Be sure you take notes. Then send her on her way.

If she keeps on with her rumoring behavior, she needs to be confronted, and perhaps disciplined. Confronted, that means sitting down face to face with her if you're her coworker and you otherwise value her ability to do her job, and confronted and disciplined if you're the boss. If she is spreading a particularly disturbing rumor, question her very carefully about where she is getting her information. Make some notes and then go and talk to her 'sources' just to make sure they really were her sources. You may get varying stories from these 'sources' but usually it's likely that the rumor has no bearing in reality, and the 'sources' are unwitting dupes in this case. Then you need to confront the monger herself once again. You don't have to name names or repeat word for word what you heard from the sources, because you don't want to be the cause of a rift among office personnel, and you sure don't want to get stuck in the middle of a 'he said—she said.' But make sure she knows that you know she's dealing in half-truths and falsehoods.

You're (most likely) not a psychiatrist so you don't have the skills to get to the bottom of her problem, but you at least stand a chance of getting control of her mouth in the office. As I said, not a pleasant thing to do but sometimes necessary.

<u>Rumor Mongers Workspace</u>

Someone in your office who really gets into spreading malicious stories:
Is there a pattern to the kind of rumors he spreads?
If yes, describe the kinds of rumors you most often hear from him:
Is there a particular person he seems to whisper about more than others?
If yes, what is it about this person that seems to irritate the rumor monger most? Don't name the person, please.......
What's your plan for dealing with him the next time a rumor gets to your ears?
Who are his usual 'sources'?   How will you go about gathering the real facts of the story?

What will you say to him when you confront him?

This one is serious enough to need an action plan if he has been spreading rumors around for a long time. What will your plan look like?

In other words, what do you want his new behavior to look like?

1.

2.

3.

4.

How long, what time frame, will you give him to correct his behavior? Why?

How will you monitor his effort to correct his rumoring behavior?
1.
2.
3.
4.

What will you do if the rumor is about your boss?
How will you handle your coworker in this case?

Notes to Self:

Snoops & Tattletales

OK, this one's for the boss. You're the new boss and you've just inherited the office snoop/tattletale. You know, the one who runs to you just to tell you – behind closed doors, of course – who in the office has what problem of the moment.

Who in the office is having an affair with who else in the office.

Who in the office fudged the figures a bit on her last expense report.

Who has showed up late to work three days in a row.

Who's having children problems at home that carry over to the office.

Who's about to leave his partner.

And on and on and on – but never out in the open, always in a 'sidebar' just to you. This is usually stuff you don't want to know in the first place because it's not causing anyone any really significant problems.... except for you, when you have to hear it over and over and over. And you are forced to spend time wondering where in the world he picks up all this useless information, when he could be spending that time actually doing his job!

There are a couple of steps you can take here. First, after the third or fourth tale passed on to you, you could say something like, "I can understand your concern about George, but I think I'd rather let him come and tell me what the problem is. He knows I'm here and he can come and see me any time. Let's give this one a rest. I don't want to turn the office into a rumor mill, so I'll just wait for him to come and see me directly. But thanks for your concern."

If that doesn't work, and all else fails, one thing that works every time is just to cut the whole deal short. Just say, "John, you know, I just don't want to hear about that. Thank you." And walk away.... Works every time!

Snoops and Tattletales Workspace

So, which have you got, a snoop or a tattletale? Or both?
Is there a pattern to the snooping or tale telling? If yes, describe it:
Is there a particular person who gets the brunt of the tattling? If yes, what do you think it is about that person that sets off the tattler?

What's your plan for dealing with him the next time he stops you in the hall with a finger to his mouth to tell you something juicy?
What are some of the kinds of things you could say to make the snoop quit accosting you with information you don't want to hear in the first place?
    1.
 	
    2.
 	
    3.
 	
    4.
 	
    5.
 	
    6.

Something to think about: what, if anything do you need to do for or with the person who is the recipient of the tale telling?

Notes to Self:

Special Cases: Yellers

Yellers are a whole different kind of problem from other kinds of DPs, in that everyone within hearing distance knows what's going on with them. They aren't the kind of DPs who work sneakily behind your back or just make barely audible snide shots. Yellers want to make sure *everyone* knows how unhappy they are. But there are some things you can do to work successfully with screamers.

The green scaly demon who's your boss. You know, the one who just loves to get in your face for no particular reason, especially in public, and in front of *his* colleagues. There's a personality problem here that you aren't qualified to diagnose, and you shouldn't have to. These are the screamers of the world. For some reason screaming is a kind of normal tone of voice for them. These people do exist and no one in the office really knows why they fly off the handle like they do, but they do and in this case he or she is the boss. The biggest problem here is that you rarely see it coming so you're caught completely off guard. So what do you do?

The first thing you need to know is that yellers yell mostly because they want attention rather than a true solution to their problem. One of the best things you can do in this instance if you're stuck listening to a screamer and can't walk away (no fading into the woodwork here!) is do some serious listening. If you listen just a bit: ask yourself what's the real problem the yeller has? You will probably be able to figure that out. What's *really* bothering her? If you listen carefully enough you can usually figure out what's the real reason for the yelling, and it usually has nothing to do with you personally, even though you might be the current, unlucky, target for the vitriol. If you think that's the case, wait till the yeller takes a breath and then say something like, "OK, I think what you need to do is_____" Or, "Can I do_____ to help you here?" Or can you help me understand _____?" Whatever you do, DON'T try to respond to every insult hurled at you. Don't start trading insult for insult. Hers don't really mean anything and you can wind up suffering if you try to keep up insult for insult.

What you *can't* do in this case, for obvious reasons, is yell back.

Some things you *can* do are:

Focus on the business at hand and don't get sucked into emotional language yourself. That's hard but take a couple of deep breaths before you respond and stick to talking about the task or the problem and not on the yelling boss. Then give it up for the moment. Most likely the boss's colleagues are as embarrassed as you are.

Then at the first opportunity, like as soon as the meeting is adjourned, ask to see the boss in her office as soon as possible. And tell her that you completely understand the importance of the task at hand, that you have completed 7 out of 10 steps, and that you have a right to civil treatment. You might also say something like, "You know, trying to make a fool of me in public won't get the job done any better or faster. I am already about to get the project completed. And I will have it on your desk by_____." If at all possible say this in a casual tone. If these efforts fail, document, document, document.

Now if you *are* unfortunate enough to have a boss who's a yeller, and you're today's target, sometimes your best response is just to suck it up and outwait him. After he is through yelling at you, your best bet is to ask for a private meeting to discuss the issue or problem that caused the outburst in the first place. Make sure the boss understands you really want to understand his expectations and you're not interested in one-upmanship.

There's a caveat here (and a number of other boss problems): be wary, be very wary, of going over your boss's head even if she is a screamer, or a bully. In most cases, who do you think will 'win' here? If at all possible, do what you can to handle the situation in your department.

Sometimes all you need to do with a yeller is simply *lower* your own voice when you are talking to him. That forces him to really listen to what you're saying. It also keeps you from going deaf!

If your yeller is attacking you over the phone, and, trust me, this does happen, forget just hanging up. BAAAAD political move! Even if you're dealing with a co-worker and not your boss, if you hang up, boy, do they have ammunition to use against you! If you really can't stand it a minute longer, tell the yeller you've got a chore to do and you'll call him back in _____ minutes. That gives you time to gather your wits and may also give the yeller a chance to calm down so you can resume your conversation at a normal decibel level. But be sure you call him in the time you set.

There are, unfortunately, occasions when you have absolutely nothing to do with the yeller's rage. Unfortunately, you just happened to wander into the line of fire, or as we used to say in one of my previous jobs, it was your turn in the barrel for the week. The yeller's problem is nothing to do with work; it may be something to do with home, a child, a spouse, and sometimes you can derail that train just by offering a sympathetic ear and not offering any advice. Sometimes people just want to tell their story.

Special Case: Yellers Workspace

Someone in your office who's a yeller:

Is there something or someone that seems to set him off?
If so, what?

If you could yell back at him, without fear of repercussion, what would you say?
Go for it!

Your plan for handling an outburst during a meeting or other public occasion:
1.   2.   3.   4.

Your plan for handling an outburst during a telephone conversation:
1.   2.   3.   4.

Your plan for meeting with this DP:

1.

2.

3.

4.

Notes to Self:

The Chronic Time Policeman

The chronic mean guy in your office/department is a lovely soul to deal with. He's the boss or department head who makes unrealistic rules, and just loves to punish anyone who violates them for whatever reason whenever he feels like it.

He sets unrealistic, perhaps nearly impossible timelines, for a major presentation. It's one of those, "I want this on my desk tomorrow at noon" situations. And it's already 3PM. You work way into the evening and then the next morning. When you approach the boss about 10 AM and tell him it's just impossible to complete this presentation in his timeframe, if he wants it done right, he blames you for not being able to meet his deadline! Then you get written up for not meeting timelines appropriately.

Or, suppose you managed to get the presentation done right on time. You hand it to the boss and he reviews it. And he manages to pick out three minor flaws in an otherwise excellent product. So you need to go around once more and fix the problems.

Either way, you feel like you've lost by going around in circles.

My suggestion, with this type of boss is:

- Listen to what he wants done.
- Give it a minute or two to turn around in your mind before you leave his office.
- Tell him you appreciate the fact that this is a very important task and you'd like to come back in 15 minutes to review the various pieces of the presentation – show him a sort of outline.
- Come back and go through the steps you've got so far and tell him that a really good job on this will require more than the eight hours he's allotted you. You need to get the charts and diagrams designed and get them into a PowerPoint presentation, along with the appropriate narrative.
- Tell him you can get as far as Step 6/8/5 by noon tomorrow, but you would appreciate 2/3/4 more hours to get it just right. After all, (gentle reminder) if the Big Boss is the target for this presentation your boss will want to look good, and he will want time to go through the presentation before it becomes public.

Remember to keep the focus on the presentation, not on personalities-his or yours. You both want the job done right and it's in both your best interests to take the time to do it right.

If this happens more than once you need to handle yourself the same way each time. You may be able, by being calm and organized, to convince the boss to schedule out such work earlier than he has in the past. I've seen this calm way of dealing with this type of boss work a number of times.

The Chronic Time Policeman Workspace

Who is/are the time police in your office?

What's his particular time problem?
What most often sets him off?

How does this behavior impact you and your coworkers?

What's your plan for dealing with a task with a difficult time frame?
1.
2.
3.
4.
5.

How comfortable are you working with short turnaround times?

Dig out your Worry Plan and think about all the negatives if you don't get your task done in the boss's timeline.

Now go back to working on your task.

Dig out the Worry Plan once more and write down and/or edit.

Now go back to your task.

What kinds of factual things can you say if you don't happen to get the job done 'on time'?
1.
2.
3.
4.
Notes to Self:

The Cons

There are a couple of kinds of con artists you might find in your office.

The first is the person who is very fond of promising things for you if you, in return, will do something for her. Does this sound like the old fashioned 'I'll wash your hands if you'll wash mine'? Usually this is a task your DP doesn't want to do herself in the first place. And most likely, her promise gets broken more often than not. So what do you do when her promise gets half broken--she starts but doesn't finish her part of the task--or gets completely broken once too many times--she comes to you with an excuse for why she just couldn't get the traded task done at all?

Well, first acknowledge to yourself that you'll most likely have to keep working with her anyway, colleague or boss. So get smart. The next time your DP says, "I'll do this for you if you'll do that for me," get it in writing! E mails confirming your agreement are wonderful here. Or those pink telephone sheets, dated with the day and time of the conversation on them. Don't do things for someone else just because they've promised you something. That's a slippery slope for sure! Because if the part of the task you were assigned doesn't get done, even though you 'traded' it to someone with the best of intentions, guess who ends up looking inept?

The other kind of office con artist is the one who loves to bend the rules and recruit 'help' from you and others in the office. She gets a specific assignment from the boss that she has no interest in doing, so she farms out bits and pieces, or a lot, of it to the kind folks-you-who are always so helpful. The problem here is that if she gets caught handing out mini assignments, and something goes wrong, you go down with her. This DP operates on the theory that if she doesn't give you time to think her idea through you will jump at it, especially if it sounds good on the surface.

Don't fall for her faulty logic. *Don't* offer excuses for why you don't want to be part of her scheme. *Don't* get into an argument. You *can* offer help-legitimate help, that is. Can you think of some alternative that goes by the book? If you can, offer several suggestions, making sure they're all on the up and up. Ask questions about the assignment. The more questions you ask, or suggestions you make, the more likely your con woman is going to just fade away. She doesn't want you to take any time to think, so that is exactly what you do.....

The Cons Workspace

Someone in your office you think is good at conning people:

What kind(s) of cons does he most frequently engineer?

How do his cons affect the atmosphere in your office?

What's your plan for dealing with him the next time you think he's trying to con you?
1.
2.
3.
4.

How will you monitor his part of a group task to keep from being conned?

Notes to Self:

The Dumper

You work with someone who loves to dump on people for just about everything. You know, the person who always dumps on your ideas in a department meeting or in front of several of your coworkers, or in front of your boss.

You have to do a little thinking about this one, because frequently the dumper will pass off negative comments as humorous if the dumpee takes offense. The problem is that it is *not* humorous; that's just an excuse, a defense mechanism, if you will, to keep the dumper from getting into trouble with too many people.

She loves to put you down no matter how successfully you complete tasks, or, conversely, she loves to dump on someone else *to* you. The problem with dumping, especially when you're on the receiving end, (the dumpee) is that even if you've done a remarkable job on an assignment, the out loud dumping can put just a fraction of doubt into other people's minds about how well you've really done. That's *not* a good thing for you, because remember, perception is reality, and if it happens enough times, people will eventually begin to look at you a little sideways.

There are two things you can do if this fits your case, and interestingly enough they are opposite from each other, but either one will work.

One thing you can do is let this coworker in on your idea before you publicize it. That might sound counterintuitive but that gives her some time to dump on you in private and gets some, at least, of her criticisms out of the way before the departmental or office meeting where you are supposed to bring your idea out. But it also gives her time to buy into the idea if she ends up thinking it's a good one and she'd like to claim part of the credit. Trust me, sharing some of the credit sure works better than being dumped on in public!

The opposite idea, a good go-to idea, if the first idea doesn't work, is to try to build a behind-the-scenes coalition of other coworkers who do believe in the idea. You might want to talk to people individually or in small groups around the coffee pot, for instance. Once you've garnered some support from these coworkers, in a public meeting you'll already have a lot of vocal support for your good idea.

The Dumper Workspace

A Dumper in your office?

What form does her dumping usually take?
When is she most likely to dump on someone in public?

Who does she usually dump on?

How does her maliciousness impact you and your coworkers?

Have you ever tried to call her out about her snarkiness?
If so, what did you do?   Did it work?

What's your plan for dealing with her the next time she dumps on you?
1.
2.
3.

What's your plan for dealing with her the next time she dumps on someone else *to* you?
1.
2.
3.

Notes to Self:

The End-around (or, Just Leave Me Alone till I Can Retire)

What do you do when you have a colleague or boss who does an end-around to pretty much every question she is asked, by pretty much anyone? This is the person who is usually the long-timer who just wants to survive long enough to collect a pension. He usually has a very clean desk, and no phone or e mails to return because he farms those out to someone else to handle. As a matter of fact, his desk is so shiny he can see his reflection in it! Usually he farms pretty much everything out to someone else to handle. If he's the boss, he feels entitled to hand off assignments. If he's your coworker, he hands off assignments he's been given to the kind people who like him and don't mind taking on extra responsibilities. Or he doesn't complete tasks at all until they get handed off to someone else for him. He's just trying to keep out of any controversy, any problem, and keep his nose clean. So he does nothing because if you do nothing you can't actually make a mistake!

What you can do here is to ask questions of him, whether he's a coworker or the boss. What you do is say something like, "Boss (or Jim), do you need more information from me to answer that question (finish that task)?" Or, "Did I make some kind of mistake, and that's why you can't answer the question (do your part of the assignment)?" Or, "I can't do the next step of this job till I hear what you want me to do."

With these types of questions you don't sound accusatory, but you do get the message across that you're not getting the answers you need in order to proceed with your task, or you're not getting the numbers you need, or you're not getting the protocols you need, and you're not able to move forward till he moves. And, as usual, document your attempts to get help from him. You're not trying to sabotage his career here, you just need help, and if your assignment falls flat you need some proof that you've done all you can to get it to work.

And there is no doubt he will make it to retirement in spite of you!

The End-around (or, Just Let Me Live till I Can Retire) Workspace

Is there someone in your office who seems to have already retired?

How does he 'relax' in the office?
In other words, how do you know he's already retired? What do you see day to day?

If he's the boss, what kinds of actions can you take to protect yourself from a do-nothing?
1. 2. 3. 4.

If he's a coworker, what kinds of actions can you take to protect yourself from a do-nothing?
1. 2. 3. 4.

What kinds of documentation make sense to you to keep?
1.
2.
3.
4.

Notes to Self:

The Exploding Colleague

You have a colleague who is always on top of things, works wonderfully hard, and is usually right on target, but she has a temper that only occasionally explodes all over everyone around her, for no reason that you can identify. She can blow your hair backwards but then she's as calm as ever. She's worth working with because she's so good at what she does, but these explosions are as hard to fathom as they are hard to take, and may eventually cause her to lose her job.

First, determine if her anger really has a cause that you can help overcome. If she's angry with someone or some situation in the office, you can probably help her. Let her know that *you* know she's angry. Say it out loud: "I see you're angry." Then ask, "What's the problem? What's upsetting you?" Once you get past this point, just keep reflecting back to her what she's saying. So, for example, "You think no one listens to you?" Or, "you think we don't ever like your ideas?" Or, "You think you always get the impossible jobs?" Keep reflecting until she has kind of worn down and has worn out most of her anger. Recognize that this kind of anger can be verbally abusive and is often VERY loudly expressed. Reflective listening is an old technique that psychologists used, and probably still do, to defuse a situation that may otherwise turn out badly, by repeating to the person what she has just said, over and over, until she begins to hear for herself what she's saying.

If you're fortunate enough to be her friend – or her boss, actually – then you tell her something like, "We'll work out some of these things together, but I'll tell you that I won't put up with a lot of shouting, swearing, and stomping around the office. Other people in the office don't need that, and it's unacceptable to blow up like that from now on."

<u>The Exploding Colleague Workspace</u>

Someone in your office who explodes occasionally:

Is there something in particular that sets her off?
If yes, what situation usually does it?

What are some specific reflective questions you could ask this colleague the next time she explodes?
1.
2.
3.
4.

Notes to Self:

The Persecutor Boss

Just in case you haven't got enough problems in the office, here comes the new boss, and in a couple of weeks, or maybe, if you're lucky, a couple of months, you realize that every time you have a conversation with her, she's putting you or someone else down. She is giving the same person/people the nasty little tasks all the time. You eventually start picking up on this and start saying to yourself, what's up with this? There are the barely heard nasty little zingers like, (under breath) "Oh, for heaven's sake, here's the complainer again...." Or, "At least you had the brains to come and ask me, not like James, who just rushes in and then figures out his mistakes later." What?

She's rewritten the office rules, without consulting anyone in the office. In some businesses that's her absolute privilege, but redoing rules solo is a real problem.

However, the problem is not necessarily with the rules, if they make any kind of sense at all. The problem occurs when the boss 'enforces' these new rules without any sense of logic. She enforces the rules in what turns out to be a really cruel manner. Suppose one of her major rules is that no one leaves the office before 5:30 PM. That's doable, but when your child falls off the playground slide at 3:30 and needs a doctor visit immediately, she says something like, "Well, it doesn't sound that serious, and if I let you go early, I'll have to start excusing everyone early for the smallest reason."

Or she says, when she refuses your request to leave early, "Well, why did you send him to that daycare center in the first place? Don't they supervise the children on the playground? Let *them* handle it." Logical? There are two interrelated concerns with this boss. She's enforcing this rule illogically and actually judgmentally. Are you made to feel like a poor parent and a poor worker at the same time? Double zinger!

This is also a person who just loves to ask for other people's opinions on any subject and then shoots them down loudly and in public, just because she can! You've been given a task by this boss and asked to put together a 10 minute presentation to the whole office on how to solve a problem. You get into the office meeting, do your thing, and the boss immediately says something like, "Well, that'll never work because it's too expensive/ not thought through enough/we don't have the personnel/it's not a very good idea....." So all the work you've done is down the drain. Time and time again until you wonder if it's even worth it.

What you need to spend a little time thinking about is that this is a very angry person, who may have a lot to be angry about. Her anger may really have nothing to do with you and your colleagues, it may be a home issue or a personal finance issue or a child issue, absolutely nothing to do with her profession. However, you are having to deal with the fallout from her anger, whatever its reason. Frequently, when a person feels like she can't control one situation, emotion is going to spill out somewhere else. In this case, it's misdirected anger aimed at people she *can* control.

There are some things you can do, though.

In the case of the snide little put downs, do *not* be drawn into adding your own comments, either positive or negative. Those will eventually come back to bite you either with the boss when you vociferously defend another person over and over again over her objections, or by siding with the boss against someone you work perfectly well with. Think about this: if the boss is putting down someone else in your presence, what do you think she's saying about you when you're not around?

In the case of an unrealistic rule like the 5:30 thing, you may very well be able to negotiate: if I leave now I will come back and put in the two hours I owe you as soon as I get my child seen to. I'll leave you an email of my time in and out this evening. Or tell her you'll be in an hour early for the next two mornings.

These are perfectly reasonable responses to this kind of boss. Unfortunately, there are bosses who won't bend regardless. In this instance you have to do what you have to do. You need to see to your child. Unless you are putting someone in the office in some kind of danger, you leave to get your child. Then you take up the problem with the Big Boss, your boss's supervisor. But wait till you have cooled down a bit, so you don't sound just like your boss!

Write yourself some notes about your conversation with your boss, including the 'counteroffer(s)' you made. Note specifically what the problem was with your child and what you did about it. Take these notes with you to the Big Boss. Be sure to state carefully and clearly that you're not trying to get anyone into trouble but that, in this case, it was an emergency that as a responsible adult you needed to handle immediately, and the situation in the office was not allowing you to do that.

Don't make it personal; don't start in on the boss, if you'd like to keep your job; keep your focus on the unfriendly *situation*. If you stoop to the boss's level and she gets censured by the Big Boss, guess who's going to feel the repercussions down the road? You need to remain neutral on personality problems of your boss, and open a conversation on perhaps revising the rules. Chances are, this is not a boss who will stay around long, because her rigidness will do her in, not just with you, but with your whole office.

The Persecutor Boss Workspace

Persecutor higher up?
In the interest of self- preservation, just say yes or no......

Can you tell where his anger is coming from?
Is there an office situation that seems to be causing it? If so, what?   Does the anger seem to be coming from an external source? Can you identify it?

Is there a particular instance or behavior that sets off the persecution?
If yes, what is it?

Is there a particular person that sets of this behavior (let's hope it's not you!)
If yes, what about this person sets it off?

What's your worst case scenario with this boss?

What's your plan for the next time you come in for some higher up persecution?

1.

2.

3.

4.

What are you going to document if you need to?

1.

2.

3.

4.

5.

6.

This one is difficult. What's your long term plan for dealing with this boss?

When he attacks me next time, I'm going to:

The next time he attacks someone else in front of me, I'm going to:

The circumstance that will cause me to go to the Big Boss:

The documentation I will take with me:
1.

2.

3.

4.

Can I negotiate with the Boss?

If so, how?

If I'd like to keep my job, I'm going to:

And I'm going to avoid:

Notes to Self:

The Rescue Problem

People who study human behavior talk about 'conversation triangles' in situations where there are more than two individuals engaged in a conversation. Most of the time, those conversations go along smoothly and end smoothly. But a problem can occur when one of these triangle conversations contains a persecutor and a 'persecutee' and a rescuer (you?).

The 'rescue conversation' occurs when a Difficult Person is verbally beating up on a co-worker. You come along and try to rescue the person being persecuted. Be aware, however, that any time you 'rescue' one person from another, the DP will invariably see you as a persecutor, and will, in turn try to make you her next victim. And the person you have rescued will probably not think you're doing her any favors either, because the existing problem has not been solved, just pushed out of sight. This conversation could be the result of what psychiatrists call a 'dependency relationship. The persecuted is dependent upon the persecutor actually mistreating her, and then she has something to complain-long and loud and to a sympathetic audience-about.

If you're not the rescuer, how do you recognize the 'perpetual rescuers' in your office/department? They can sometimes cause as many problems within an office as the DP can. If you think you are the constant rescuer, pay attention. Do you:

- Often do things for people that they could just as easily do themselves, or for themselves just as well, if not better?
- Offer help just to keep other people dependent on you? That's a tough one; you may have to search your conscience on that one.
- Find yourself willing to take the boss's abuse for the good of the cause rather than let others stand up for themselves?
- Frequently find yourself feeling guilty when you cannot solve someone else's problem for them?
- A lot???
- Find yourself saying to yourself more than once a week, "I really don't want to get into this, I hate this stuff" right before you wade in?

Well, guess what? You're really not helping the persecuted person. You're not helping her learn to solve her own problems. And the worst part is that all dependent relationships eventually lead to hostility, probably by all the other parties involved. There's a reason Native Americans have a saying that translates to something like: when you save my life, *you* owe *me*.....

There's one major thing for you to do here, if you work with someone who is a chronic rescuer, or if you yourself are the chronic rescuer: separate your problems from the problems of the persecutor and the perscutee (is that a word?). That's hard, but listen to the conversation before you jump in with both feet. Does it have anything at all to do with you? If it doesn't why in the world are you getting involved????

If it's not your problem turn around and walk away. That may be hard to do, if you're a rescuer, but take a minute to think about what you may be getting into. Think about what the persecutee whines about most. How many times in the past have you already 'saved' him? And, as Dr. Phil says, how's that working for you????

If you're the boss, separate the two combatants without offering any help or suggestions. Then *call each one into your office separately and have a conversation about whatever the problem* was, if it is relevant to the work site.

If it's a personal problem unrelated to business, for heaven's sake stay away from it! You can certainly tell coworkers to take it somewhere else, and you can be a sympathetic ear, but if you get embroiled in someone's personal life you may really be in for it later! In this case, 'sympathetic ear' means do some reflective listening, repeating or rephrasing what the persecutee is complaining about until he eventually begins to hear himself. Taking some time to converse with him in this way will usually calm him down. However, if you get into the conversation and it turns out that the problem is a personal one-spouse, child, parents- you need to simply say something like, "I'm so sorry you're having problems with your teenager. I hope it works out. Now, let's go back over this report and look through the charts, and you tell me what information you need to finish it." That's all you need to say to steer clear of getting involved where you don't want to be.

The Rescue Problem Workspace

Someone in your office who frequently needs to be 'rescued' from other people:

What does her 'rescue me' behavior look like?

From whom does she most often need to be rescued?

What kinds of circumstances most often get her into a 'rescue' situation?

How do you normally respond to her?

Now let's look at yourself:
In general, how often do you: Often do things for people that they could just as easily do themselves, or for themselves just as well, if not better?
Offer help just to keep other people dependent on you? That's a tough one; you may have to search your conscience on that one.
Find yourself willing to take the boss's abuse for the good of the cause rather than let others stand up for themselves?
Frequently find yourself feeling guilty when you cannot solve someone else's problem for them? A lot???
Find yourself saying to yourself more than once a week, "I really don't want to get into this, I hate this stuff" right before you wade in?
What's your plan for interacting with her the next time she comes to you for rescue?

Notes to Self:

The Sneaky Ones

What if your DP is a back stabber and/or a gossiper? In this case, if you've been chosen to hear a particularly salacious piece of office gossip, your best bet is to be right up front with her and tell her you're not interested in office gossip, period. The faster you steer the conversation to something innocuous the better off you'll be. Because you know that if someone else in the office gets wind that you've been discussing him behind his back, even if all you're doing is listening to the gossiper, guess whose goose ends up getting cooked.....

Sometimes this DP is not easy to spot at first. She gets her kicks from doing all her dirty work by plotting and scheming behind the scenes. She likes to think of herself as the puppet master. What you discover is that she really has no interest at all in creating or promoting a positive atmosphere in the office. The best thing you can do here, once you finally catch on to what's going on with this person, is to dissociate yourself from her. Don't let your name ever be mentioned in the same sentence with her name. Let her know in pleasant but specific terms that you will not be migrating over to the "Dark Side', her side, any time soon.

On the other hand... Remember that old saying about keeping your friends close and your enemies closer? Once you figure out that there's a schemer operating on the sly behind your back, you might be wise to try to convince her to come over from the Dark Side and into the light. You don't have to let on that you know she's been scheming, but once you've opened a dialogue, she will most likely get the message that you are onto her.

There are also schemers who, for their own particular reasons, will try to set you up at every opportunity. And it's probably not just you; it's anyone they feel like setting up on this particular day. This is all behind your back, of course. She may want to take major credit for a lengthy and complex report that you have been working on with her. Or she may want to get even with you if you have received a lot of credit for an excellent presentation and she feels she's gotten short-changed. Your answer here is to make doubly sure you've covered all your bases, done all your homework and met all your deadlines. If you consistently take care of these things, there's no way this schemer can really get you.

Some DP's are wonderful at creating and breaking up 'alliances,' almost like they were contestants on "Survivor." Get to know, and then pay attention to, what factions are around your office, who's allied with whom, who's on the outs with whom. This may be a situation in which you are better off playing the game than removing yourself from it. You love your job but you'll never be able to keep it if you don't slide into the fray. Who's in your own alliance? Who do you know doesn't like you or want to work with you (I hate to break this news to you but, yes, there's always someone)! Who seems to be playing around with the DP? These DPs are the ones who are expert at playing both ends against the middle. Pay attention to who is nattering with whom in the corners. You are much better off keeping the main thing the main thing, as the saying goes so just watch from the sidelines as much as you can, but get into the fray when you feel truly threatened. This DP may well eventually find herself in a one person alliance – her own – after pretty much alienating everyone else in the office.

The Sneaky Ones Workspace

A schemer in your office?

Who's in her 'alliance'?

Where are you in relation to this alliance?

Who's in *your* alliance?

Who in your office does *not* want to work with you?
Why do you think he/they don't want to work with you?

When you are assigned a common task with him/them, how do you handle yourself?

Think about the last time she tried to set you up.

What happened?

Now, reimagine what you would have said that would have taken her down a peg without getting you into a direct confrontation?

Her:

You:

Her:

You:

Her:

You:

Her:

You:

Her:

You:

How would you end the conversation?

What's your plan to make it very hard for her to set you up again?
1.
2.
3.
4.
5.

What's your plan for dealing with her if she tries to draw you to the "Dark Side" with her?
1.
2.
3.
4.
5.

Is there ever an occasion in which you would join another faction rather than fight against it?
If so, what would make you think that it was more worth joining in this instance?

What will you do in future to make sure you cover all your bases when dealing with her?
1.
2.
3.
4.
Notes to Self:

Verbal Abuse

Difficult people are frequently verbally abusive. By spewing out long and loud abuse, they think they can pass off the blame for their problems and failures to you, because you will get lost in all the verbiage. And guess what? It frequently works!

These are the bosses that yell-sometimes literally or sometimes in a low threatening tone-at you individually or at the whole office or department. For example: the whole office has been responsible for putting together the various parts of a grant proposal, which the boss has parceled out. Due date is approaching and the boss has called a meeting to go over the parts and write a summary. But before you even get to the summary you start to hear, "Who wrote this section? This doesn't even respond to the question! This goes so far off it's not even useful! The writing is terrible! I don't even understand this! And while I'm on the subject, I've never liked the way you people put these things together. We never get grants because you don't do your research in the first place! Your work on these things is pretty shoddy! But, then again, it's usually pretty shoddy! You expect me to sign off on this piece of junk? You expect me to risk *my* reputation on this? Go back and see if you idiots can at least *answer the questions right, huh?*" And on and on and on and on. Meanwhile, the whole office is sitting and slinking down in their chairs at this abuse, because they think they are bad at what they do and this is all their fault.

Hmmmm. What do you do? In the first place, this is your boss for good or ill. If she only breaks down like this on occasion, you might suspect she's under great pressure from *her* boss, so it's in your best interest to ask something like, "Boss, if you'll help us out here, we'll get this corrected and turned around by tomorrow at quitting time. Give us a couple of ideas about what you want to see changed." No sarcasm, please. And then go do it. There's no future in fighting back; you only lose. And before you leave this meeting, ask for a specific time and place to go through the document again. Reacting in this manner does two things: it defuses the boss, because she's got to think about the draft in a focused way at least for a few minutes-which gets her out of the yelling circle-and it reassures her that you are all really on her side. That never hurts in the long run. And, if you all collectively think you've really done an accurate job on answering the questions in the first place, go back to your cubbies, clean up the writing, double check your facts, and get ready to defend yourselves at the next meeting. And good writers will say that it never hurts to reference the question in your answer to it, which will add to your defense at the next meeting.

If your boss is one of those DPs who frequently gets into this circular reasoning-loudly and long(ly), that's a different problem. These are the bosses who just want to assert their authority because they are more important than you are, and you come to realize that she gets into this mode even when there's absolutely nothing wrong with what you're doing. You can basically do the same thing: ask for references to what the boss thinks she wants changed, suggest a time to meet again to go over changes, go back to your cubbies, make minimal or cosmetic changes, and then go on with your business.

The point is that getting upset by being personally insulted by a boss who verbally abuses everyone, a lot, on a kind of lower key, is probably a waste of time, and easily fixed. However, if the verbal abuse involves profanity, threats, blasphemy, you write it down! Date and note who's there, and go straight to the boss to talk about this problem, if you feel you can. If you really feel personally threatened, you need to hotfoot it to your Human Relations Office to talk about this. There are laws about this kind of verbal abuse.

Suppose, however, you're the boss and you're dealing with an employee who, it comes to your attention, is verbally abusing his coworkers, and seems to be getting them to 'help' with his assignments through what is really intimidation. This may be a person who thinks he can get away with it because he has seniority in the organization, or he has advanced degrees, or he has the selling record for the company; therefore, he's better than they are. As the boss, you gather documentation on the verbal abuse. Don't go looking for 'tattletales' or sneaks; do keep your ear to the ground about what's going on out of your presence in the office. Talk to individuals who have been the victims of the abuse to gather facts: what was the conversation about, when did it occur, what were the circumstances, what did the victim do as a result of this conversation? You write up your notes and keep them on file. Depending on the policies of your organization, you might need to submit your notes immediately to HR. Otherwise keep a running file and after about the third time the abuse happens to the same person, call in the victimizer, and go over your notes. Questions to ask: do you remember this conversation? What were the circumstances of the conversation? What were you hoping to accomplish in this conversation? What did you want this employee to do as a result of this conversation? Are you aware that that was really verbal abuse? Remember to practice your reflective listening even here. You may find that this DP is not even aware of his tone and language. However, chances are, he is. This meeting serves to put him on notice-you're aware of what's going on.

By the way, notice that you don't ask him, "*Why* are you talking this way to Joe?" The answer you'll get is basically the same answer you'd get from a 10 year old, who's stolen cookies from the cookie jar: "I don't knowwwwwwww." That doesn't help anyone.

What you do: put him on an action plan. No more than three steps, but tailor them to this person. The three steps might be: 1. when you talk to Joe (or Sue) at any time make sure someone else is in the office with you; 2. do not go into Joe's office for the next three months; if you want to talk to him, ask if he can sit down with you in the break room (or wherever, in public); 3. keep notes of your conversation with Joe for the next three months. At the end of three months I'd like to sit down with you again and see where we are. Set the date and place and time for the next meeting now. And, remember, this doesn't work if you don't follow through........

Verbal Abuse Workspace

A verbal abuser in your office?

Who bears the brunt of the abuse most often?

Is there a pattern that typically sets off the abuse?
If yes, what do you see?

What's your plan for dealing with him the next time the abuse starts?
1. 2. 3. 4.

Remind yourself: what is it you're *not* going to ask him? And why not?

If this is someone who reports to you, the next time you get wind of him verbally abusing someone in the office, what are three Action Plan steps can you design for him?
1.
2.
3.

How will you monitor him during the Action Plan?
1.
2.
3.
4.

What will you do if he does not successfully complete the Action Plan?

Notes to Self:

Resources:

Worksheets, Scenarios, Blank Plan Sheets

Worry Check Sheet

I'm going to worry about:

_____
_____
_____
_____
_____

I'm going to worry for exactly _____ minutes, no more and no less.

Worries/worst case scenario:

1. -
    _____
    _____
2. _____
    _____
3. _____
    _____
4. _____
    _____
5. _____
    _____
6. _____
    _____
7. _____
    _____
8. _____
    _____
9. _____
    _____
10. _____
    _____
11. _____
    _____
12. _____
    _____
13. _____
    _____
    _____
14. _____
    _____
15. _____
    _____

Second round worries:

I'm going to worry about this and add, subtract or change what I have already written.

And I'm going to worry for exactly _____ minutes!

1. _____

2. _____

3. _____

4. _____

5. _____

6. _____

7. _____

8. _____

9. _____

10. _____

And now what am I going to do about it?

1. _____

2. _____

3. _____

4. _____

5. _____

Of course, if you have more worries just copy this page and keep going. Happy worrying!

My Action Plan

Pick ONE behavior or attitude this DP exhibits that really bothers you. Focus on ONE thing at a time. If this person exhibits more than one difficult characteristic, use one Workspace for each characteristic.

Remember that this Work Plan focuses on you and what you want do when faced with this person.

Think about a Difficult Person you know. What is the ONE thing about him/her that really grates on you?
Describe:
How would you LIKE him to respond to you?
Describe:
Work Plan:
1. I'm tired of him being:
2. So I want him to:
3. When he_____:
4. I want him to:

5. The next time he_____:

6. I am going to:

Notes to Self:

Practice Scenario One

Bob and Jim work in the same department. Jim is a new employee. Bob has worked at the company for a long time.

Bob and Jim do the same job, have the same job title, and have to work together.

Bob likes to do things the way they've always been done. He's very vocal. And because he's been there so long he thinks he knows how to do things. And he tells others how to do things, whether they ask or not.

Jim tries hard to follow company rules. Jim is a very quiet man; he doesn't talk much. He has conservative and has traditional values.

Employees must clock in within five minutes of the start of their shifts. They are supposed to clock in at their own buildings, but there isn't any way to check this.

Bob always clocks in at another building so he won't be marked as tardy. He always gets to his work station at least 10 minutes late.

At least a couple of times each week, somebody asks Jim where Bob is.

Jim is tired of covering for Bob, but he's kept it inside himself for a long time.

Finally, one morning, Bob is 20 minutes late. Jim has to cover for him for the 20 minutes.

When Bob finally shows up, Jim tells him he refuses to cover for him anymore.

Bob says, "Hey, I clocked in. I've been doing this way for years! As long as you don't say anything to anyone else, nobody will ever know. So just shut the %#$*& up and do your job."

Bob and Jim start shouting at each other.

You walk in just as it looks like Jim is about to slug Bob.

What do you do?

Practice Scenario Two

At the Smith Auto Parts Company people work in teams. And when a particular belt line doesn't have enough parts, the extra workers are sent to other lines to help out.

Marie is a complainer. She whines all the time.

One day she is sent to a neighboring belt line for the day. George, a coworker, greets her. He smiles and says, "We're glad to have you as part of our team today. We enjoy having people from other departments help us out."

Marie snaps back, "This isn't what I was hired to do. I'm only here because I have to be."

George tries to explain the work on the line, but every time he says something, Marie whines.

George decides to try to make the best of it, but on the morning break, several other team members complain to George about how much Marie complains.

Later in the day, the line stops while more parts are brought in.

Marie whines, "This is stupid. Why can't management get it right? I don't care if they pay me to sit here and do nothing."

When the line gets up and running again, Marie whines that she was just getting comfortable, "and there's only an hour and a half left in the day anyway."

George tells her that they'll need her back on this line again tomorrow because the customer is in a hurry for the order. Then she can go back to her own department and do her job.

The next day, as soon as Marie arrives on the line she starts whining again. By lunch time, the rest of the team is just about in revolt.

You walk in just as George is literally being backed into a corner by upset employees.

What do you do?

Adapted from the Kent State Education Department

Notes to Self:

Partnership Agreement Template

This is a template you can use for yourself or with someone else after you have come to an agreement to 'solve' a DP's problem.

- Goals:

- Behavioral Outcomes:

- Ground Rules:

- Parameters for the future relationship:

- Steps for achieving goals:

- Time frame:

- Checkpoints:

- Feedback?

<u>Work Plan</u>

1. We've got accountability in place for both/all parties.

2. Our expectations are clear for both/all of us.

3. We've defined our goals clearly.

4. We each/all know our individual responsibilities.

5. We've decided how often we should sit down with each other.

6. We've both/all agreed on who should call our meetings.

7. We've designed our criteria for what success looks like.

8. We've developed a good strategy for handling roadblocks to our progress.

9. We've set a date for completion of our process.

References:

In case you want to do some more research on your own

1. Bell, Arthur H. , Ph.D., and Dayle M. Smith. <u>Difficult People at Work: How to Cope, How to Win.</u> MJF Books. 2005.
2. Brinkman, Dr. Rick, and Kirschner, Dr. Rick. <u>Dealing with People You Can't Stand: How to Bring Out the Best in People at Their Worst. 1994.</u> McGraw-Hill Companies, Inc. 3rd ed. 2012.
3. Business Management Daily. <u>Difficult People at Work.</u> 1998.
4. Cava, Roberta. <u>Dealing with Difficult People at Work and at Home.</u> Smashword. 2004, 2011.
5. Cavailoa, Alan A. <u>Toxic Coworkers: How to Deal with Dysfunctional People on the Job.</u> 2000
6. Deblauwe, Tony. <u>Tangling with Tyrants: Managing the Balance of Power at Work.</u> HR4Change Press. 2009.
7. Flaxington, Beverly D. <u>Understanding Other People: The Five Secrets to Human Behavior.</u> Motivational Press. 2010.
8. Furlong, Gary T. <u>The Conflict Resolution Toolbox: Models and Maps for Analyzing, Diagnosing, and Resolving Conflict.</u> John Wiley and Sons. 2005.
9. Gee, Jeff, and Val Gee. <u>The Winner's Attitude: Using the "Switch" Method to Change How You Deal with Difficult People and Get t he Best Out of Any Situation at Work.</u> 1st ed. McGraw Hill. 2006.
10. Johnson, Steve. <u>The Office Politics Exercise Manual: the Seven Laws of Surviving Freaks in a F#@&*d Up Workplace – Limbering Up for the Fight of Your Life at Work, v. 10.</u> Johnson Publishing. 1st ed. 2012. Kindle Edition. 2012.
11. McGrath, Helen, Ph.D., and Hazel Edwards, Ph.D. <u>Difficult Personalities: A Practical Guide to Managing the Hurtful Behavior of Others (and Maybe Your Own).</u> The Experiment. 2010.
12. Moore, Mike. <u>How to Cope with Difficult People at Work.</u> MJM Publishing. 2011.
13. Perfect Phrases Series. <u>Perfect Phrases for Dealing with Difficult Situations at Work: Hundreds of Ready to Use Phrases for Coming Out on Top Even in the Toughest Office Conditions.</u> 2008.
14. Samson, Alain. <u>Be Positive or Else Stay Home!</u> Self-published. 2011. Kindle edition. 2012.
15. Scott, Ginny Graham, Ph.D. <u>A Survival Guide for Working with Humans: Dealing with Whiners, Back-Stabbers, Know-It-Alls, and Other Difficult People.</u> AMACOM 2004.
16. Solomon, Muriel. <u>Working with Difficult People.</u> Prentice Hall Press. 2002.
17. Topchik, Gary S. <u>Managing Workplace Negativity.</u> AMACOM. 2000
18. Wofford, Monica. <u>Make Difficult People Disappear: How to Deal with Stressful Behavior and Eliminate Conflict.</u> John Wiley & Sons, Inc. 2012
19. Ury, William. <u>Getting Past No: Negotiating in Difficult Situations.</u> Random House Publishing Group. 1991.
20. Ury, William, Roger Fisher, and Bruce Patton. <u>Getting to Yes: Negotiating Agreement without Giving In.</u> Penguin Group, USA. 1992.

About the Author:

Kathy Tuten has been an educator for more than four decades. She was a teacher, a curriculum coordinator, an assistant principal, a principal, and a school system level instructional officer, all in her first professional life.

In her second professional life she taught at the University of North Carolina, where she was an assistant director in the nationally known and respected Principals Executive Program. In this program she taught principals, assistant principals, district office personnel and school boards the tenets of leadership: what makes an exceptional leader on the local and national level.

In her third professional life she worked for the State Education Superintendent of South Carolina in the capacity of the Director of the Office of School Leadership, again working with educators to encourage the practice of better leadership styles and methods.

At her retirement from the State level, Kathy decided to challenge herself in a relatively radically different field of interest. She worked for Pearson Education in their staff development division, creating and managing sophisticated dashboards that allow school systems to manage many forms of their individual school and district data to improve teaching and learning within their districts. An additional part of that position was working with Pearson's sales staff in making connections with school people

Kathy's has conducted seminars with an incredibly wide variety of adults who have themselves worked in interesting and sometimes difficult circumstances. Her most requested seminars have been on how to work with difficult people in an office setting. This is an especially important skill to have in these times of shrinking job markets and job pools.

Thus this workbook that doesn't just teach what works, but requires introspection on the part of the users, so that they can use the information to improve their work lives.

Kathy as a B.A. in English Education from Pennsylvania State University, an M.Ed. in Education from the University of North Carolina, Curriculum Specialist Certification, Supervision, and Advanced Administrative Supervision from the University of North Carolina, and has pursued post-graduate studies at the University of North Carolina.